Digital
Branding

Digital Branding

A complete step-by-step guide to strategy, tactics and measurement

Daniel Rowles

KoganPage

LONDON PHILADELPHIA NEW DELHI

First published in Great Britain and the United States in 2014 by Kogan Page Limited

2nd Floor, 45 Gee Street	1518 Walnut Street, Suite 1100	4737/23 Ansari Road
London EC1V 3RS	Philadelphia PA 19102	Daryaganj
United Kingdom	USA	New Delhi 110002
www.koganpage.com		India

© Daniel Rowles, 2014

The right of Daniel Rowles to be identified as the author of this work has been asserted by him in accordance with the Copyright, Designs and Patents Act 1988.

ISBN   978 0 7494 6995 5
E-ISBN 978 0 7494 6996 2

British Library Cataloguing-in-Publication Data

A CIP record for this book is available from the British Library.

Library of Congress Cataloging-in-Publication Data

Rowles, Daniel.
    Digital branding : a complete step-by-step guide to strategy, tactics and measurement / Daniel Rowles.
        pages cm
    ISBN 978-0-7494-6995-5 (paperback) – ISBN 978-0-7494-6996-2 (ebk)   1. Internet marketing.
2. Branding (Marketing)   I. Title.
    HF5415.1265.R688 2014
    658.8'2702854678–dc23
                                                                    2014004434

Typeset by Graphicraft Limited, Hong Kong
Print production managed by Jellyfish
Printed and bound by CPI Group (UK) Ltd, Croydon, CR0 4YY

*This book is dedicated to my wife Susana,
my daughter Teresa and my son Charlie Bear.
I have one word to say to you, mousosaurus's.*

CONTENTS

FOREWORD

The business environment is rapidly changing and the fast-paced world of digital media is a real challenge for organizations of all types. What we need to think about when building and measuring brands is increasingly complex.

At the Chartered Institute of Marketing (CIM) we see time and time again that practitioners and those studying business of any type (whether they consider themselves marketers or not) need a better understanding of the digital landscape. That landscape is changing incredibly quickly and our idea of branding needs to adapt accordingly. Knowledge of both the strategic impact and the tactical issues around digital branding will become increasingly important, particularly as social media and mobile technologies have more and more of an impact.

Daniel has worked extensively with CIM, helping our members and customers to navigate their way through this exciting and fast-moving environment. He is a respected authority on all things digital and as such is the ideal guide for your digital journey.

Anne Godfrey, Chief Executive, CIM

Introduction

'**B**rand awareness' is an excuse used by marketers when they don't know the value of what they are doing. If they are asked the question 'how does that social media campaign impact the business?' and the answer is 'it's good for brand awareness', then it generally means they haven't got a clue.

Most of us don't sell things online with a credit card payment facility. Most businesses have sales transactions in which the sale takes place somewhere other than our own website. It is therefore very hard to work out what the return on investment (ROI) is for the digital activity we carry out (particularly when we involve social media). 'Brand building' or 'brand awareness' are terms that are often used as the objective for work where the true objectives are not clear.

This book aims to demystify what brand actually is in a digital world, to show what it is doing for the bottom line, how it can be achieved and, most importantly, how it can be measured and improved.

This book will help you to build a robust framework for planning, implementing and measuring the effectiveness of your digital campaigns. This will mean that you are able to develop a measureable digital strategy based on clear objectives.

How to get the most out of this book

The book is split into three key sections:

1 Digital branding in perspective

This part explores what we really mean by branding, and how this has completely changed because of digital marketing channels and technology. We explore what we really need to understand in order to be able to measure the effectiveness of our digital campaigns.

2　The digital toolkit – the user journey and digital channels

Part Two looks at the practicalities of using all of the digital channels and tools available to us. We explore topics such as social media, mobile marketing and search optimization, while connecting them all up to the user journey.

3　Digital brand strategy and measurement

In the final part we build a process for developing a digital strategy that can be implemented, measured and improved. We look at a robust framework for measuring all elements of our digital activity, including how to calculate the ROI of social media. Most importantly it will be made clear how the strategies we develop are related to our business objectives.

To accompany this book there is an online resource of related materials including case studies, templates and tools. You can also get all the latest on digital branding by visiting

http://www.targetinternet.com/digitalbranding

PART ONE
Digital branding in perspective

Introduction

Let's start by saying what digital branding isn't. It isn't about logos or visual identity and it certainly isn't about celebrity endorsements and big sports team sponsorships. What digital branding is really about is the sum of our online experiences. These online experiences may be influenced and impacted by logos and sponsorship, but we need to understand branding to be something much more than visual identity.

Branding has fundamentally changed because of digital media. Digital has led to two-way communications between brands and consumers – social media means that we can now talk directly with the brands that we use every day. In fact, most communications via digital media don't even involve the brand any more and are now directly between consumers. We only need to look at review websites such as TripAdvisor to realize that what consumers are saying about us is more important than what we are saying about ourselves.

A traditional view of branding

When I say that branding isn't about visual identity or logos many people will be shocked. I'm not saying that these things are not important, but what I am saying is that they are an increasingly small part of a much more complicated picture. Your logo and the visual aspects of your website design will certainly impact on a consumer's perceptions of your organization, and they mustn't be overlooked, but the reality is that we now experience things in our connected world in a much more complicated way than previously.

The number of different online touchpoints (points at which we are interacting with a topic, product or organization either directly via something such as a website or app, or indirectly via a search engine results page or a social media discussion) we make before making a purchase are increasing. We are seeking more sources of information and are assigning trust differently. Gone are the days when marketing consisted of putting your product into the hand of a celebrity in a shiny 30-second TV commercial and thinking your efforts were complete.

This shift to dialogue rather than broadcast means that the traditional approach to branding is no longer sufficient. We need to understand how search, social media and mobile are impacting our target audience's perceptions of us and how it is impacting their likelihood of buying our products. We also need to do this in a measureable way.

It's all digital

Although this book is about digital branding, it is not only digital that creates your brand. It is every experience that your target audience has of you. From your call centre employees' tone of voice through to the type of paper you print your business cards on. The fundamental shift, however, is that all of these things are tied together by an online experience.

What do you do after you see a TV or print ad? Well, according to the Internet Advertising Bureau (IAB) nearly 50 per cent of us will use our mobile devices to search for a product of interest (IAB, 2013). What do you do after that frustrating call-centre experience? Up to 40 per cent of us will go online to vent our frustrations (NewVoiceMedia, 2013).

The reality is that our mobile devices are bridging the gap between our online and offline experiences, so that even broadcast media needs to carefully consider the online interaction it will cause.

Brand awareness as an excuse

I started this book by saying that brand awareness is a phrase that is often used as an excuse to justify digital activity that doesn't have clear objectives. Let's take an example. Many organizations have Facebook pages. Yet most organizations have no idea as to why they have a Facebook page.

There is a body of research called the Social Media Benchmark, a series of studies carried out by the Chartered Institute of Marketing looking at how organizations of all types are using and being impacted by social media. What is abundantly clear from each stage of this research, however, is that the majority of organizations are not using social media effectively, but they are doing more of it!

We will look at this in more detail in Part Two, Chapter 5. In this part we will explore what digital branding really is and how it means that branding has fundamentally changed.

Business to business

When we talk about brands and consumers it is easy to assume we are talking about a business to consumer (B2C) situation. In fact, all of the principles we are discussing equally apply in a business to business (B2B) environment as well. As the potential customer in a B2B scenario, we are still an individual going through a decision-making process. Although the buying cycle may be different and the decision-making process motivated by different factors, we can still map out and understand how digital branding is having an impact.

In reality, the process of mapping the impact and value of what we do online in B2B is even more apparent because the majority of B2B purchases are actually made offline and we need to understand what role digital is playing in making that sale.

What digital branding really means

A traditional view of branding says that a brand is: 'Name, term, design, symbol, or any other feature that identifies one seller's good or service as distinct from those of other sellers' (*American Marketing Association Dictionary*, 2013). In fact, the word *brand* is derived from the Old Norse word *brandr*, meaning 'to burn', and was used in reference to marking cattle by burning the owner's brand onto them.

This idea of branding has been developed over the years to factor in a far more extensive set of considerations. As well as this idea of visual identity we may also consider the thoughts, feelings, perceptions, images, experiences, beliefs, attitudes and so on that are associated with a brand. This set of considerations builds up our *brand image*, and we may also talk about our experience of a brand as our *brand experience*. The best way of thinking about it, in my opinion, is that brand is the *personality* of something.

How digital has changed branding

If you could only get a feel for someone's personality by them telling you things about themselves, we may end up with a very shallow understanding of them. We may also have difficulty believing in the personality that has been constructed – and we may start to question the motivations behind what they are telling us about themselves. That is exactly the situation of commercial branding that uses broadcast channels such as TV. A personality is sculpted and then we are told what the personality is. We don't get to discuss, engage with and really understand the true personality.

Digital media now means, however, that the conversation is no longer one way. I can challenge, ask questions and develop a truer picture of the brand. I can see through a sculpted brand and start to see it for what it truly is. This can be a scary thing for many traditional brands. It can also be a huge opportunity.

Brand democracy

I was originally switched on to the idea of brand democracy by a good friend of mine and renowned inspirational speaker, Jonathan MacDonald. Brand democracy is the idea that your brand isn't what you say it is, but rather the sum of what everyone else says it is. This has huge implications for not only how we manage our brands, but also on how we need to change the very nature of our organizations.

You can read Jonathan's original, and often challenging, thinking at the website: **http://www.jonathanmacdonald.com**

Global soapbox

If brand is essentially the personality of something, digital media gives us the ability and opportunity to understand the *true* personality of something. We can then use that understanding to help guide us in our decision-making processes.

This is a great opportunity from a customer point of view. For example, it means that instead of being put on hold for an hour when phoning a call centre and having little choice but to tolerate it, I can now go straight to one of many social media channels and make my frustrations very clear and very visible. I now have a global soapbox with access to all of the other potential customers out there, and I can impact a global organization's brand in a way that was not possible before (or, at least, was incredibly difficult). That highly visible complaint then becomes part of other people's brand perception (fairly or not) and suddenly the years of building a brand can be tumbled very quickly. This is a very much changed environment for businesses to operate in – if they ignore this change then it can lead to problems.

This ability to engage with and research into a brand can also be looked at from an even simpler point of view. Perhaps I am researching buying a car or a B2B service. I can now do a lot of research and inform my decision before I speak to the car dealership or service vendor. When I do make this final step I am far more informed and have developed a fairly in-depth perception of the brand before I engage directly with them. In fact, from information I glean online I may have opted out from even considering certain brands. That information may have been on a third party website in the form of a review or comment from someone I have never met, but I may trust it over the voice of the brand itself.

Brand perception

I did a search for the word 'Comcast' in YouTube – you can read the results below. Comcast are a very large provider of cable TV and internet connections in the United States. By searching for their brand name I got a very interesting array of videos that may have an impact on my perceptions of that brand and may influence my likelihood of buying a service or product from them.

The first video is someone claiming to have a technique for getting cheap deals on Comcast services. The second video, with over 1.7 million views, is of a Comcast engineer having fallen asleep on someone's sofa because they had needed to call their own call-centre and had been on hold for over an hour. The third video is someone getting very annoyed with a Comcast employee on the telephone over a billing issue. The fourth video is, wait for it, the story of another engineer falling asleep in someone's house! The fifth video is of someone claiming to have a poor quality cable installation from Comcast. The sixth video is of someone leaving a positive review of a Comcast product.

We'll explore how we can deal with (and avoid) issues like those that arise from negative videos such as the first five listed here. We will also learn, when we explore the idea of brand advocacy, how the sixth video can be extremely valuable.

Social media fail

This fast-changing environment and the slow pace of businesses to adapt to it is leading the social media disaster stories that we see on a daily basis on the internet. Some of those stories will be highlighted later in the book in order to see what we can learn from them, but they generally have a number of things in common. Most social media disasters demonstrate a lack of knowledge of how to practically use a particular social media channel, or show a belief that the brand can manipulate the channel in some way and get away from this need for authenticity and transparency. The other common theme is that of failing to understand the changed role of the brand in this two-way conversation. All of these themes will be explored in Part Two when we look at social media.

Traditional brand metrics

Traditionally, brand has been measured by asking questions and trying to judge what someone thinks of a brand, and trying to work out what this means in regard to potential sales.

There is a wide range of different ways of looking at this, but generally we would take some sort of sample survey of our audience and see what their attitudes were before and after exposure to some form of marketing. This survey would ask a range of questions, and there are lots of different approaches, but fundamentally we would look to answer the following questions:

- Are you aware of the brand?
- Do you like the brand?
- Do you intend to buy the brand?
- If you have purchased, do you intend to do it again?

Essentially we are assuming that if we can get more people to answer positively to each of these questions, we are likely to get more sales.

This can still be an extremely valid process when effectively integrated into an overall approach, and we will explore this in more depth in Chapters 15 and 16.

Sum of all experiences

Essentially, digital branding is the personality of our organization, service or product created by the sum of all experiences that an individual has with that brand. This still includes things such as visual identity, but now also includes much more important and influential touchpoints such as social media interactions and online reviews. Your logo may make you recognizable, but it is your overall brand that decides what I remember you for.

Clarifying touchpoints

If we are defining digital branding as the sum of all experiences that an individual has with a brand, it seems straightforward to use the term 'touchpoint' to refer to one of these experiences (as we already have done). We do need to be careful, however, of the definition of a touchpoint. A touchpoint is often interpreted as some sort of engagement or experience with a marketing channel created by the brand. This idea of a marketing channel can be expanded to include everything from packaging to telephone calls. Clarification is needed, though, when we go beyond these brand-controlled experiences to things like word of mouth and social media engagement. Very often these types of touchpoints will have no involvement with the brand at all, for example when a consumer reads an online review. Yet this is still a touchpoint and probably one of the most important of all touchpoints.

Points of view – Allister Frost

Allister works with a wide range of global organizations helping to plan and implement their digital marketing strategies. He was previously head of Digital Marketing Strategy at Microsoft, he lectures at Middlesex University and is part of the Social Media Advisory Forum.

The days of being able to neatly segment our marketing communications into 'traditional' and 'digital' buckets are behind us. Today there's only one marketing and all of it is digital to some extent. Even press advertising, a bastion of marketing convention, is not immune to this change. Print ads that fail to quickly connect their promise with entry points into consumers' digital lives no longer deliver their full potential in an increasingly digital world.

It's incumbent upon everyone in the marketing industry to embrace online channels and discover better ways to help consumers find, enjoy and share great content that supports your business goals. This means moving beyond conventional 'spray and pray' advertising approaches, and creating great branded experiences for customers at every stage of the buying cycle. After all, a brand is little more than the sum of all the things people say about it. The modern marketer's task then is to ensure that the conversations that surround our brands are factual, favourable and easily discovered through whichever channels our customers choose to explore. That's where the new return on investment comes from, the volume of online chatter that positively influences your brand sales. It's time for a brave new beginning, welcome to the digital world!

Allister Frost, founder of Wild Orange Media

Focusing on value

02

With all this talk of brand perception, social media engagement and changing business environments, it's easy to get distracted from the business and marketing fundamentals that are essential to our organization's success. This is especially true when the environment we are working in is changing so quickly, and it is easy to be distracted by what is new and 'shiny' rather than what is effective.

Fundamentally we need to be clear on two key things: first, we need to always have clear sight of what our business objectives are and to focus on how any marketing activity we are carrying out is connected to this. Second, we need to understand our target audiences' objectives so that we can align what they want with what we are offering. We need to understand their motivation. Everything else is really secondary to these two key points – and it is always good to get back to these fundamentals from time to time.

Bridging the gap

Traditionally when we consider business objectives and target audience objectives, when these two things overlap we can see value. Value for both the business and the target audience (see Figure 2.1).

However, the reality of this in a digital environment is that this potential value is not enough. If I want you to engage with me online it is not enough for my product or surface to just provide value. I have to give you a reason to want to engage, to leave feedback about my product or service, and to generally create dialogue.

FIGURE 2.1   Aligned business and user objectives create value

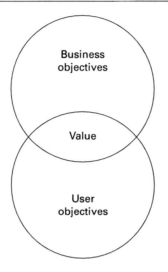

This is where digital branding comes into play. Digital branding can bridge the gap between our business objectives and what my target audience actually wants to engage with (see Figure 2.2).

FIGURE 2.2   Digital branding bridges the gap between business objectives and target audience objectives

Value proposition

Value proposition is defined in a number of different ways by different people, but fundamentally it is a promise of value that should be appealing to our target audience – and that they believe will be delivered. It may be a promise of value in a single product or an entire organization. Your digital branding allows you to communicate this value proposition.

Let's take a look at a few examples from different markets to make things clear as to how all of this fits together.

Business to business service

If I want you to buy a complicated B2B service from me, I need to do a number of things, but most of all I need to give you the content you need to help you make a decision. This means I need to map out all of the stages of the buying cycle that you will go through and make sure that all of the different questions you need answered are covered. In most B2B situations, the potential customer won't engage directly with a potential supplier until they have decided exactly what they want.

This may mean educating the audience on some topics even before they fully understand what I am offering. If this is an item that has a long buying cycle, or is a very occasional purchase, I will also need to engage with the audience when they are not actually in the process of buying yet. This means I must provide value beyond just talking about my solutions.

A standard digital branding approach here is for us to ourselves position a useful resource on an industry topic and provide value through content. This could be anything from industry news, leadership articles through to in-depth reports, but the key thing is that I am providing value outside of just talking about what I do.

We need to measure the effectiveness of this content and what impact it is having in driving sales.

Consumer packaged goods

Many consumer packaged goods (CPG) are things like groceries and toiletries and are generally not highly differentiated. That is, many CPG aren't all that different to their competitor's products, so branding is very much what helps differentiate them. In fact, this is the market in which a traditional approach to branding was really developed. The problem in a digital world is why would I speak and engage online about detergent or confectionery?

This is where digital branding can bridge the gap between what a consumer wants to engage with and what an organization wants to talk about. By broadening the conversation and understanding our value proposition, we can find topics that a user will engage with. As examples: Skittles engage users with fun and quirky humour via Facebook – this creates repeat exposure and affinity with the brand; Dove use the theme of 'real beauty' to engage the audience and stimulate conversation – this creates exposure to the brand along with aligning the brand with positive topics. We need to measure the effectiveness of this social media engagement and understand what impact it is having in driving sales.

Complex consumer products

When we are buying a more complex consumer product, such as a car or a technology product, the process is actually very similar to the B2B process, even though that product may be purchased online.

A potential customer needs to understand the market and options available to them. We need to understand where they are in the buying cycle in order to provide the right content, and we may need to try and engage with them before they are even considering purchase, in order to build awareness and likelihood of purchase.

Charity funding

When a charity is seeking donations and potentially a long-term commitment to monthly donations, engagement is essential. It is essential so that I feel motivated to donate initially, but also so that I don't decide to stop donating and cancel my payment at some point.

Understanding motivations for donating becomes essential, and working out the value exchange that is going on can be very powerful. Social media allows for powerful personal connections, and by allowing individuals to portray themselves to their peers as they would like to be perceived, a charity can use their digital branding to provide great value for their audience, ie the charity can provide the mechanism via social media that makes the person donating look generous, caring or any other characteristic they would like to be associated with.

A note on luxury brands and boy bands!

With all this talk of value proposition and online touchpoints, you may be thinking of examples where this doesn't apply. The first and most obvious one is that of luxury brands. I have heard the argument many times that a luxury brand cannot be defined by a simple marketing process. Yet I would argue that exactly the same principles apply.

Your perception of a luxury brand is simply made up of all of the online and offline touchpoints that you have with that brand and its products. We have already said that digital branding is the set of digital touchpoints that shapes our opinions, and this is essentially no different.

Quite often, brands are developed over a number of years and this involves spending millions on advertising and placement in order to achieve the set of touchpoints to make you feel a certain way about that particular brand. You may see a celebrity using a product, see a brand in a certain high-profile event, or see a series of print ads that associate the brand with a luxurious lifestyle. These are simply touchpoints that are crafted to appeal to all sorts of human emotions and shape how you feel towards a brand.

Where this can really be seen as failing is with things like boy bands (go with me on this one!). My 11-year-old daughter is a big One Direction fan and she will buy any piece of tat that has their picture on it. Surely this isn't about delivery of value proposition through marketing touchpoints? You guessed it, I think it is.

The reality is, her opinion is based on multiple touchpoints, and many of those come in the form of the most effective type of touchpoint, peer to peer recommendation. One thing that boy bands have always had is an army of fans willing to engage and say positive things about them to other fans. I'm not suggesting there is no more to it than this, but clearly the value proposition (whatever they represent to their fans) is extremely well aligned with what the fans want, and the extensive series of interactions they have around the 'brand' are highly effective.

Recently the BBC looked at what it meant to be a fan in a digital world in a piece titled 'Super-fan 2.0: Why loving One Direction can be hard work' (BBC, 2013). They concluded that social media not only gave fans an opportunity to discuss their favourite topic, but also to get noticed by the bands they adore. How do they do this? By growing the level of social following to be an influencer of the target audience. They have essentially made themselves influencers, and as any traditional PR approach will show you, influencing the influencers is essential.

Rather than boy bands being an exception to the rule, what I think they demonstrate is the power of a highly engaged and connected audience, and that is exactly what digital, and particularly social, media can offer us. It actually means we can build a brand in record time – and that the years spent building many of today's luxury brands may become a thing of the past.

It all comes down to content

All of the above examples show how we can use various digital channels to provide value, as long as we fully understand our target audience and their user journey. Digital branding is the sum of experiences that we have online and it relies on the provision of value. The provision of that value will generally rely on some form of content, which may be something that educates us around a topic and builds our trust, or content that we can share with our peers to make ourselves perceived in the way we would like to be perceived. Even when we are dealing with products that would generally generate little engagement, we can drive engagement through appropriate content and smart digital branding.

Digital branding is the sum of experiences we have online and relies on the provision of value.

To do this well, however, we really need to focus on the user journey and see how we can provide value in order to influence the decision-making processes involved in purchasing anything. Understanding that user journey is exactly what we will look at in the following case study.

CASE STUDY   Heinz – Grow Your Own

This campaign was launched in March 2013.

Background

People everywhere love ketchup, but not many realize how many actual tomatoes are used to produce it. Heinz asked us to help educate its core audience of mums and kids that ketchup isn't just made – it's grown.

Objectives

We had to educate a nation about a product that has been around for over 130 years, by communicating Heinz's key message to consumers that ketchup isn't just made – it's grown using fresh, healthy tomatoes. We had to do this in a new, up-to-date way that would resonate with Heinz's core audience – mums – and allow us to engage with them while at the same time encouraging them to get their kids involved in the campaign.

Strategy and execution

We decided that talk was cheap – the best way to get cut-through with consumers would be to *show* them what ketchup is really made of. So we took a hands-on approach, by getting people all across the country to grow their own tomatoes.

The campaign was activated through the Heinz Tomato Ketchup Facebook community, with a dedicated 'Grow Your Own' hub where fans could enter their details in order to be sent their own pack of tomato seeds, completely free of charge, courtesy of Heinz.

We created a 'Tomato School' to help fans find out how Heinz grows its tomatoes, and how they fit into the Heinz Tomato Ketchup recipe. Fans could also learn how best to grow their own tomatoes, from planting the seeds to nurturing blooms to picking their fully grown tomatoes.

Throughout all the stages of growth, fans were able to post their own photos in our 'Greenhouse Gallery', giving inspiration to other would-be tomato growers and also giving them the opportunity to win exclusive Heinz Ketchup branded garden goodies. We also created an interactive 'Grow Your Own' game, where people could 'virtually' grow their own tomatoes by reacting to changing conditions – factoring in temperature, bird invasions, watering, weather conditions – all to keep the tomatoes alive and flourishing.

Results

'Grow Your Own' was Heinz's most successful social media campaign to date. While it was led by social media, it went much further than simply creating an app or providing a clever gimmick.

The 'Grow Your Own' game was played 59,203 times, up 25 per cent on Heinz Ketchup's previous Facebook game. There were around 300 photos uploaded over the course of the campaign, with mums and kids making up the bulk of the entries with some really imaginative and inspiring growing techniques. During the campaign, the Heinz Tomato Ketchup Facebook page gained 66,396 new likes and the campaign reached over 11 million people on Facebook alone, with over 180,000 engaged Facebook users.

Most importantly, we had a whopping 31,627 packets of seeds ordered from all over the UK – thousands of green-fingered mums and kids all learning about Heinz Tomato Ketchup, its ingredients and, of course, growing their own tomatoes!

Comments

Although this is a really great example of a creative campaign being well implemented, we are still lacking any direct evidence of increase in sales or ROI. As it is fairly clear that this is a successful campaign, and that an increase in sales or ROI would be the case, let's see how we could demonstrate this.

From an ROI perspective we can look at this in a number of ways. First, we could look at the audience size and engagement period and then calculate the cost of achieving this same level of attention using a traditional channel such as TV.

Alternatively we can try to look at the impact that the campaign directly had on sales, and this would require some level of surveying about purchase intent. Had we changed people's opinion of the brand in any way? Had it impacted any of the traditional brand metrics of awareness, consideration, preference or loyalty? I think it is likely that most of these metrics would have been impacted, but without sampling and asking questions we don't know for sure that this is the case. We'll explore this type of surveying in Chapters 15 and 16.

Considering the user journey

03

So far we have discussed the idea of digital branding being the sum of all of your online experiences. We have also mentioned several times that managing this effectively requires understanding the user journey, so let's map this out in more detail and look at some of the tools that can help us along the way.

Multichannel marketing

The reality of all marketing is that it generally isn't just one thing that makes you buy a product or choose a supplier. Generally it is a huge range of factors that make you prefer one brand over another, choose a particular supplier or buy a particular product. Digital branding is all about understanding this process and making it measurable.

As marketers we can model, measure and use all sorts of tools to try and understand this buying process – and this is where digital marketing has its greatest strengths. We have access to more data and more ability to measure the user journey than ever before.

However, the missing piece in this measurement puzzle can be the interaction between online and offline marketing. Quite often mobile can act as the bridge between the two, yet we still face some challenges with this. The journey is very likely not to be a linear one: many channels and types of content may be revisited several times and we may not have any visibility on some of the steps in the journey. However, we still have a better view than we have ever had before, and with a little planning we can fill in the gaps.

User journey examples

Let's take a look at two real-world user journeys – B2B and B2C – all the way through to purchase and consider how different channels are working together.

Business to business example

I need a new hosting company for my business website. I'm responsible for the website's reliability and I have had some bad experiences previously, ending in my website being down, which left me feeling both frustrated and embarrassed. This buying decision is primarily motivated by risk mitigation, but I also need to make sure that my website will be fast and that any provider will give me the opportunity to expand and improve my web offering, so I need flexibility and performance. This is not a decision I will make without being well informed, and the user journey is made up of multiple steps, including but not limited to:

- Doing numerous searches for suppliers.
- Reading online reviews of these suppliers.
- Signing up for newsletters from each of these suppliers.
- Asking opinions on LinkedIn and Twitter from my social network of their experiences.
- Completing several diagnostic tools to understand what kind of hosting I actually need.
- Reading websites that talk about the technology behind hosting in order to educate myself about it.
- Signing up for newsletters from the sites that helped me educate myself.
- Talking to colleagues and trusted partners at unrelated events and meetings. Getting recommendations for suppliers I had never heard of and making a note on my phone.

So let's map out what is important to note in this user journey. First, that my decision is being based on risk mitigation and finding the right fit to my needs. I also need to educate myself on the topic (which is very common in B2B buying decisions).

We also need to note the practicalities of this journey. It was done almost entirely online, except where face-to-face word of mouth was involved. However, I only knew that I should search for several of the suppliers because I was already aware of them due to some other offline interaction at previous trade shows. Also, much of the time I was reading and educating myself I was actually offline as I had no internet access (I was either on a plane or on a train with poor connectivity).

So what does this tell us about our digital branding? Well, our value proposition needs to align closely with the ideas of risk mitigation, trust and education. So a clear value proposition aligned to user needs at the heart of any strategy would be essential for any potential supplier. The suppliers need to provide more content than just telling me how great their solution is, and I need education in order to build trust. Together these elements convey a classic example of the need for content marketing, which we'll discuss shortly.

I had relied heavily on my social network and online reviews to influence my decision, so an effective social media approach was also clearly going to be essential for any potential supplier.

As well as needing these different types of content I needed to be able to consume them in ways that suited me. And what suited me varied by time and place. I need content that will work on all of my devices.

Business to consumer example

I'm looking at what I can do with my airline loyalty points, how the process works and where I might like to go. This process is as much about enjoying the process of looking at the destinations I could visit as it is about making any sort of practical plan.

As I work through this process I will make a number of steps that may include but are not limited to:

- trying to log into my account online to see how many points I have;
- understanding the process of using the points to book flights;

- seeing how far the flights can take me – and obtaining a list of available destinations without having a particular destination in mind;
- understanding when flights are available;
- looking at the destinations, exploring holiday options and looking at the suitability for different types of travel (romantic, family, etc);
- working out the most cost-effective way of using my points, considering airport taxes and other charges.

Bear in mind that I said this was as much about fun as it was about practical planning, so this was most likely to be done in what *Harvard Business Review* call 'Me' time (*Harvard Business Review*, Feb 2013). Therefore, a lot – if not all – of this research would be done on a mobile device from my sofa. Nearly 30 per cent of all website visits to travel sites are now on mobile devices (Digital Tourism Think Tank, 2013).

I cite this example because not only is it real, but with my particular airline of choice it turned out to be nearly impossible. The key point here is that it was essential to understand the motivation of my user journey, and that was to explore, to learn and to 'mock plan'. Let's take a look at some of the issues that got in the way of this process meeting my requirements:

- main site redirecting to mobile site with limited functionality;
- no ability to go back to main website easily;
- main website not designed to work on multiple devices;
- search options not suited to my user journey of being unsure of my final destination;
- no easy way to browse availability without browsing through page after page of dates;
- no further information or recommended sites on potential destinations;
- unclear guidance on travel options when travelling with family (I will not be popular if I'm sitting in business class sipping cocktails and waving to my family who are seated in economy).

These are not just technology issues. After all, the airline had an app. They just hadn't thought through the different user journeys, and the process had been mapped to work with their booking system.

If these journeys were embraced, any airline or holiday company I was looking up would have the opportunity to engage me, re-enforce their brand and give me inspiration for future travel. Even if it didn't lead to me booking there and then, by making the process easier they could improve my brand loyalty and potential word-of-mouth recommendations.

This point of it not leading to an immediate booking is an important one and is at the heart of mobile branding. I may go through the whole flight-booking process only to drop out at the final step. This may not be because something went wrong, but rather that I was using the tools available in order to *plan* rather than make a booking. I may then go through the same process a month later and actually make a booking. I need to be able to understand this journey and attribute value to the original visit that didn't end in a sale. This is something we'll explore more and, in fact, we can solve this initially complicated-looking scenario simply by using some free web analytics software (I'm referring to something called 'multi-channel funnels' in Google Analytics).

Content marketing

Content marketing is often talked about when looking at user experience and search optimization (two things we'll look at in Part Two), but it is also very much part of your approach to digital branding. Fundamentally, content marketing is about providing useful and engaging content that is suited to the user's journey. Generally, content marketing is about providing value beyond what your direct product offering is. If we go back to my example of selecting a hosting provider, a useful focus for content marketing would have been educating the user about web technologies. A few more examples are set out in Table 3.1.

TABLE 3.1   Ideas for content-marketing themes

Type of company	Focus of content marketing
SEO agency	Digital marketing advice
White-water rafting (aimed at teams)	Team building and human resources
Alcoholic drink brand	Cocktail-making and recipes
Detergent	Family money-saving tips
Sportswear	Training and fitness tips
Business service	Thought leadership articles

Content marketing, value proposition and brand

Content marketing allows us to bolster our value proposition through digital-delivered content or services. More importantly, we have the opportunity to use digital technologies creatively to deliver this value proposition via interaction.

Table 3.2 takes our ideas for content-marketing themes and looks at how they could be applied in an interactive way.

TABLE 3.2   Content-marketing themes and interactivity ideas

Focus of content marketing	Interactive idea
Digital marketing advice	Campaign reporting tool
Human resources	Interactive HR guide with scenario planning
Cocktail-making and recipes	Interactive portable recipe book
Family money-saving tips	Coupons and location-based savings
Training tips	Training-objective progress tracker
Thought leadership articles	Interactive audio/video tutorials

All of these very simple ideas could be developed into something far more robust that would interactively re-enforce a brand value proposition. It is important to understand how this can be applied to organizations with completely different products or service offerings. A B2B service is generally a high-involvement purchase. That is, you think carefully and do some research before buying. Buying confectionery, on the other hand, is generally a very low-involvement purchase – you're unlikely to go online and compare chocolate bars before buying them! However, using digital-delivered services and content marketing can help bolster value proposition and brand positioning in both cases.

The stages of the user journey

Google have put a lot of time into investigating the user journey and trying to understand the different stages we go through when making buying decisions. Let's also be realistic here. Much of the research published by Google ends with conclusions about how their products can fulfil the requirements outlined in the research (and why not, they are a commercial organization). Putting aside commercial objectives for a moment, let's take a look at a piece of work that I think is particularly useful when trying to understand the mobile consumer.

Procter & Gamble's first moment of truth

We'll start by taking a step back in time to 2005. Procter & Gamble (P&G) published their take on what they called the 'first moment of truth' (FMOT). This was covered widely in the press and made a significant impact on their overall strategy, as outlined in the annual report of 2006 (P&G, 2006).

The idea of FMOT was that there was some sort of initial advertising push that the consumer was exposed to (which is called the 'stimulus' part of the journey in the models we will explore), but much of the actual decision-making process was actually influenced at the brief moment when the consumer was at the shelf in the supermarket (bear in mind that this model was originally targeted at what we would call consumer packaged goods (CPG) or fast-moving consumer goods (FMCG), so it looked at that specific set of potential user journeys).

They then speculated that there was a 'second moment of truth' (SMOT) when the customer purchased the product, took it home, used it and formed an opinion on it. These three steps of stimulus, FMOT and SMOT made up the traditional wisdom of how to think about marketing campaigns.

Google's zero moment of truth

Some six years later Google decided that this model was out of date and added one significant change to the model: the zero moment of truth (ZMOT). This is the step that comes between the stimulus and the FMOT. It is when we do our research, educate ourselves and compare and contrast products and services.

In a way, this is nothing new, as we always had word of mouth and asked the opinions of our trusted friends, colleagues and loved ones. What Google has suggested in this model is that the internet has enabled completely different consumer behaviour. They then continued to prove this point by carrying out a series of research that looked at how much research people did before buying different types of products and how long they took to do this. The basic conclusion was that the ZMOT was now the most influential of the now four-step marketing model (see Figure 3.1).

Limitations of 'zero moment of truth'

The ZMOT truth model can be applied fairly widely and, in fact, it works fairly well anywhere that some form of research is done online before purchase. This could be a complex and fairly long buying cycle such as a car or B2B service, or something more short term like comparing restaurant reviews online before visiting. What it doesn't work well for, though, are products such as detergent or bread. In most cases we don't go online to research these types of products before purchase. However, if we expand our idea of ZMOT to include the kinds of interactive experiences we discussed earlier in this chapter, such as engaging with content on Facebook or playing an online game, it can still be applied. Also bear in mind that with these kinds of products we may also be seeking out coupons and vouchers. This again forms part of our overall user experience.

FIGURE 3.1   Google's 'zero moment of truth'(ZMOT) model

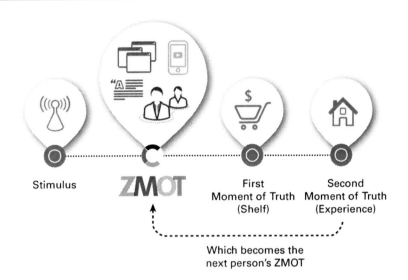

The feedback loop

Not only is this model interesting because it explores how the internet has changed our buying behaviour, it also shows a much closer connection between our ZMOT, that point when we are researching online, and the SMOT, when we have experienced a product or service. It is now easier than ever to leave reviews online that influence other consumers' buying decisions.

This feedback loop can be extremely powerful. For example, it has radically changed the travel industry, with nearly 40 per cent of consumers consulting online reviews before booking (World Travel Market, Jan 2013).

This can be a mixed blessing for businesses. I was recently consulted by a large hotel group who asked me how to deal with a major problem they had with numerous negative reviews on the TripAdvisor hotel review site. The answer, which they gracefully took on board after some initial resistance, was that they needed to improve their hotels.

You can get the full details on Google's 'zero moment of truth' (ZMOT) by visiting: **www.zeromomentoftruth.com**. Much of the research they started here is continued on their excellent 'Think With Google' site: **www.thinkwithgoogle.com**

Mapping the user journey

Now we can start to understand how we can consider each step of the user journey. What we also need to start thinking about is how we can use the different digital channels appropriately in order to achieve our goals.

In Part Two we will look at the practicalities of each of the digital channels, and in Part Three we will build a step-by-step process for developing our digital branding and looking at how we can measure it. However, before we get there let's take a quick look at the practicalities of each stage of the user journey (as set out in Figure 3.2) and how different channels can be used effectively.

FIGURE 3.2 Google's 'the customer journey to online purchase'

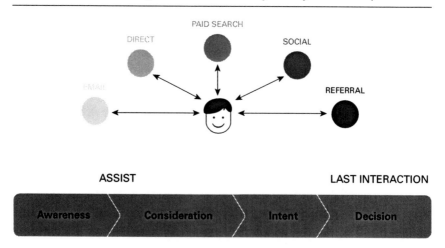

(Google and the Google logo are registered trademarks of Google Inc, used with permission)

FIGURE 3.3 Google's 'the customer journey to online purchase' in action for the B2B category in the UK

Channels play different roles in the customer journey

Biz ▼   U.K. ▼

Check out whether each channel plays more of an "assist" or "last interaction" role. The "assist/last interaction ratio" helps illustrate this behavior. You can also view paths for different industries and regions.

Legend ⬤ A channel's position on the chart is defined by the "assist/last interaction ratio." In general, ratios less than one mean the channel 2.2 acts more as a "last interaction," while ratios greater than one mean that the channel acts more as an "assist interaction." The ratios in this report have been normalized to clarify channels' roles.

(Google and the Google logo are registered trademarks of Google Inc, used with permission)

Google offer a wide range of fantastic free tools, some of which we explore more in Part Two. The tool that is most relevant to us right now, however, is 'the customer journey to online purchase' (see Figure 3.3). The tool is based on a model that splits the buying process into four key stages: awareness, consideration, intent and decision. It then looks at how different channels are more or less effective in different stages of this buying process. Interestingly, there are also significant differences between different geographic regions.

From the example in Figure 3.3 we can see that in B2B social media is most likely to be useful for driving awareness, whereas organic (the main area of search results in Google) and paid search are most likely to be the final interactions before a purchase is made.

This idea of social media as an awareness builder can be highly effective, and although it applies differently to different markets, it can start getting us to think about things in a particular way. Set out in the case study below is how my own business uses various digital channels, and what value proposition is delivered via our digital branding.

Goals and conversions

At this stage, it is worth defining some terminology that will be important throughout this book: a *goal* is something we want our target audience to do, generally on our website. This could be buying something, but it could also be the filling in of a form, downloading something or just visiting a particular page; a *conversion* is the completion of a goal.

By tying these activities back to our social media and other digital channel activity, we can start to understand how they are contributing towards our online objectives.

CASE STUDY

Company

TargetInternet.com (disclosure – this is one of my businesses).

Industry

Online learning (small business).

Location

Virtual with global customer base.

Marketing objectives

To drive highly qualified enquiries for an online digital marketing training solution, aimed at organizations with large teams to train. Lean business approach, so any approach must not require additional staff.

Their challenge

It was identified early on that the majority of TargetInternet.com's potential customers had no idea what digital marketing e-learning was, or if they needed it. It was also clear that the potential customer base was so broad in terms of different industries that an industry-by-industry approach would have been highly time-consuming and resource intensive.

TargetInternet.com operates as a 'lean business', meaning that full-time staff are kept to a bare minimum.

Their solution

Give away free educational content on digital marketing and then filter the traffic that this generates into useful business leads.

TargetInternet.com position themselves as providers of practical, up-to-date and easy to understand digital marketing training. This is achieved by using a content-based strategy to engage and build trust with an audience who may not even be aware that the service even exists.

The website acts as a content 'hub' where a wide range of free digital marketing educational content is held. A single section of the website focuses on the commercial service offered, with the majority of the website offering free content. The free content includes blogs, videos, in-depth reports and a regular podcast. On each free content page there is a call to action to drive the visitor through to the conversion page (see Figure 3.4).

Content delivers the key value proposition of credible and easy to understand content, and a series of different digital marketing channels are used to manage the sales funnel.

Social media drives awareness and sends traffic to the website via Facebook, LinkedIn, Twitter, YouTube, Pinterest and Google+. Social media activity also helps to drive search rankings by creating social signals that indicate the website's credibility.

The library of free content helps to achieve search rankings and drives search-engine traffic. It also builds trust with the target audience by demonstrating expertise.

E-mail data collection throughout the website allows for ongoing communications and the building of a clearer understanding of the target audience, as well as the individual potential customer.

Cross-sell messages then direct any interested section of the audience to a conversion page that explains the service provided and encourages the completion of an enquiry form.

FIGURE 3.4 The sales funnel of TargetInternet.com

Their results

Monthly visitors: 6,000.

Conversion rate to leads: 0.1 per cent.

Monthly leads: 6.

Conversion rate of leads to sales: 50 per cent.

What's good about it?

Each digital channel has a clear role in the sales funnel, and the complete focus on content-based marketing means that the value proposition and digital branding are very closely aligned.

Although the conversion rate of visitors to leads is low, this is an expected consequence of driving a broad digital-marketing-interested audience. Content is then used to deliver the value proposition, and sales are driven organically from an engaged audience.

The very high conversion rate from lead to sale indicates the self-qualifying nature of the conversion page. This process minimizes the need for an extensive sales team and keeps cost to a minimum.

Being able to track each stage of the sales cycle like this means that each step gives the opportunity for improvement through optimization of each channel and stage of the process.

What they said

TargetInternet.com is a lean business, meaning we focus on scaleability and keeping costs to an absolute minimum. Focusing on our digital branding means we can deliver maximum impact without needing to scale up costs, particularly around sales staff.

The focus on high-quality content means that our core team spends its time focusing on what they are good at: producing educational digital marketing content. This ties in directly with what we sell, and means that our value proposition and the digital branding we use to deliver it are completely aligned with who we are as an organization. (Susana Mascarenhas, Commercial Director)

CASE STUDY   Tipp-Ex – Shoot the Bear

Background

Up to now Tipp-Ex had not engaged online with its audience, and while they were looking to raise brand awareness they didn't specifically seek an online campaign.

Objectives

The brief as given to their creative agency, Buzzman, was 'To raise short-term brand awareness and to be on top of customers' shopping lists. To go Europe-wide and tell the story of how the product is used.'

Strategy and execution

Buzzman decided to push Tipp-Ex online with this particular campaign and used data mined from YouTube to direct the course of the ad. Having identified an ad title that would fare well on YouTube, the campaign was built around an interactive video titled 'Hunter shoots bear', with the title deliberately phrased to attract high volumes of traffic despite not having any obvious relationship to the brand.

Buzzman wanted to surprise and delight the audience, and so before the hunter shoots the bear, he reaches out of the video and uses the Tipp-Ex ad image to white out the word 'shoots' and invites the viewer to type in any activity they would like to see the bear and hunter perform.

In order to respond to this, Buzzman carried out further in-depth keyword research to identify not only the scenarios most likely to be typed in, but also the variety of alternative terms that could be used to describe each scenario. In total, Buzzman created 42 different scenes for the viewer to access, and used real time data to tell them which scenarios were most popular, giving them great feedback on their user behaviour.

Results

The video has so far had over 21 million views on YouTube, over 500,000 shares on Facebook and has been posted on more than 1,300 blogs.

Tipp-Ex noted that their 'buying attention' increased by 100 per cent and actual sales increased by 30 per cent compared to the same period the year before.

Buzzman created the campaign based mainly around the type of content that people love to view and share, and then built in the Tipp-Ex brand around it. This is a somewhat risky approach but in this case they got it just right. A nice touch was adding in NSFW (Not Safe For Work) to the title, as this had proven to make the video far more likely to be watched.

A year later the brand developed a sequel that seems to be doing just as well, with over 10 million views already – so we may see more of the hunter and bear clips.

Objectives and authenticity

04

It sounds obvious, but every piece of marketing activity that will help to build your digital branding needs to have a clear connection to your business objectives. If we are to build a Facebook page, tweet five times per day or build an iPhone app, we need to be very clear about how it is contributing towards our bottom line.

I know, for example, that by tweeting a number of times per day I will drive traffic to my website, because I link back to the content I produce. I will also build my Twitter following, because my content gets shared, and so I will have a larger audience to share with in future. This social activity will help to persuade the search engines that my website has authority, by giving it the 'social signals' it needs to move me up the search rankings. This in turn will lead to more visitors to my website because of increased search visibility. The engagement with my content drives trust and improves the perception of my site.

These may seem like great things to aim for, and they are, but in reality I'm only doing them because a certain percentage of traffic and audience can then become paying customers. Without focusing on this sharp end of the sales funnel, I am producing volume for the sake of it. After all, I can have a million Twitter followers but it doesn't necessarily mean that I'll ever sell anything.

We can spend a huge amount of time, effort and resources on digital branding, which if not properly aligned to our business objectives will not produce results. In light of this risk, this chapter is dedicated to exploring a case study of one of my favourite digital branding campaigns that ultimately failed. Something that on initial inspection seemed like a stroke of genius in digital branding, but that ultimately failed to achieve business results and was unceremoniously dumped and replaced with a very traditional approach to branding. The brand in question even produced a case study that talked about how putting your product into the hands of a celebrity was no longer a suitable approach to branding – and now they had taken a new approach, one that may on superficial inspection seem to reflect the ethos of what we are trying to promote in this book. Essentially, though, the approach used did not drive sales, and we need to understand why this was the case.

Branding for differentiation

The brand in question was Pepsi and the campaign I'm referring to was the Pepsi Refresh Project. If you are based in the United States it is fairly likely that you're aware of the project, but outside of the United States it didn't really get much coverage. When I heard about it, and watched the case study video, I fell in love. I suddenly thought that a massive brand had really got it – and I was convinced initially that it would be a success. You already know that it wasn't, but let's talk through the mechanics of what they did and look at what, on first inspection, looks like excellent digital branding (and, in fact, much of it is absolutely excellent).

Pepsi already knew that trying to differentiate on product alone was futile. Even their own video case study states very clearly that even though Pepsi and Coca-Cola taste slightly different, they are both 'brown, fizzy, soda pop'. I should mention at this time that the original description in the video was 'brown, fizzy, sugar water' – that version of the video disappeared pretty quickly!

This was a fairly bold way of approaching things. They then went on to say that you *could* put your product in the hands of a superstar in a 30-second shiny Super Bowl commercial (the most expensive TV advertising slot in the world) but that they were going to do something different.

By the time I got this far I was nearly dribbling with excitement. To tell your customers something they clearly already knew, but that had never really been admitted, was honest and exciting. Pepsi made it clear that their product was very similar to other products on the market and that they had been marketing by using celebrity mega productions. Wow, I was impressed.

Then they blew my mind. They said that the Pepsi Refresh Project would give away the $20 million they were going to spend on their Super Bowl commercials to good causes. And that the audience could select the good causes by voting via social media. I was massively impressed, and so were a lot of other people. It gained huge coverage. It was a news story in its own right. Millions of people voted. I used it as a case study at every presentation and keynote that I did for months, and I still use it to this day.

So, with this great idea, what happened next? They ended up closing it down (quietly) and moving back to a strategy of aligning with celebrities. Why? Because it didn't generate sales. We really need to understand why.

Another viewpoint

There is a lot of analysis out there on this particular campaign, and by far the best in my opinion is that by Craig Bida on MediaPost – it's definitely worth a read: **http://www.mediapost.com/publications/ article/186127/why-pepsi-canned-the-refresh-project.html**

Authenticity

I think we can sum up in a few words why the Pepsi campaign didn't work. It wasn't authentic. Now, I don't mean that they weren't donating all that cash, and I certainly don't mean that they lied in any way. What I mean is that this digital branding wasn't truly authentic with who they were.

There are a couple of telltale signs that really make this stand out. It was a project; we describe it is as a campaign – both of these things generally imply that it has a beginning and an end. For this truly to have changed things, it needed to be the start of an ongoing commitment to a value proposition around making the world a better place. The thing is, we all knew that even though this was a great project, Pepsi wasn't suddenly some sort of social enterprise or charitable foundation (they actually do have a charitable foundation and you can find what good work they do in the call-out box opposite). We knew this was a marketing campaign to make us buy more fizzy drinks. This tells us something fundamental about how digital branding has to be different to our traditional ideas of branding. A brand can't just tell us that it represents something and then assume we will believe it. The brand needs to live its values and then has the opportunity to communicate this via digital branding.

Authentic value proposition

I've stated that your digital branding is there to deliver your value proposition. What we also need to be clear on is that your value proposition has to be completely authentic. If you say that you are committed to making the world a better place, you better live by those words. If your digital branding says that you truly care about customer service, then you really better care. Everyone in your organization needs to feel personally responsible to deliver this value proposition. That is because it is a promise, and none of us like to have promises broken.

There is nothing all that new in this idea, but digital branding means that we cannot hide behind hollow promises any more. For example, consider how the public reacts when a politician who is campaigning for family values has an extra-marital affair (a timeless example) – it feels even worse when we are let down by the very person who said they understood what we wanted and shared our values.

The digital world we live in means that there are many more ways for our lack of authenticity to be exposed. This transparency means that we can build powerful brands based on real promises faster than ever before. That same transparency means that a lack of authenticity will be exposed.

Let's be fair

I want to make it clear at this stage that I really respect Pepsi for being bold enough to try the Refresh Project in the first place. I also respect their decision to can it (pun intended) when it didn't work. However, I consider that what they have replaced it with misses the opportunities that digital branding offers, but we'll see where they go next.

As for that charitable foundation I mentioned, you can find it at the link given below, but to quote Pepsi from their own website: 'Since 2005, PepsiCo, through its Foundation and divisions, has donated over $0.5 billion in cash and product to qualified nonprofit agencies working in environmental, educational, civic, arts and the health and human service fields.' That is nothing to be sniffed at. Did you know about it? Neither did I. Maybe they should have focused on that...

The PepsiCo Foundation:
http://www.pepsico.com/Purpose/PepsiCo-Foundation

PART TWO
The digital toolkit

Introduction

This section explores a range of the digital tools and channels at your disposal in order to deliver your digital branding. This is the practical hands-on toolkit that will help you understand how the different digital channels fit together, are suited to impact different parts of the user journey and to deliver your value proposition.

The guidance, tips and tools highlighted here have all been drawn from my own experience of planning and implementing digital campaigns for a wide range of organizations around the globe, from global film franchises through to chemicals that go into paint to make it whiter. The surprising thing is that most of these organizations have exactly the same problems and challenges. However, they may need to approach these challenges in slightly different ways, using different channels to achieve their desired outcomes.

In Part One we discussed the user journey; this section of the book is about selecting the most appropriate techniques to interface with that user journey in order to help create the value that we discussed.

We will also explore the idea of not making too many assumptions and making sure we always operate a 'test and learn' approach. A great example that I learnt through my own business demonstrates this well. I publish a regular digital marketing podcast, an audio show for marketers and business people generally, and as such it is a B2B podcast. As we all probably already know, generally speaking Facebook is not a place for B2B. As an experiment we launched a Facebook page for the podcast to try and test if this assumption was correct. It took little resource as we basically used the platform to post links through to the content we were already creating and to generate some feedback on this content. We had little expectation but thought it a low-cost test worth a try.

The results were surprising, to say the least. We now have nearly 15,000 people who have liked the page, engaged with our content and driven traffic back to our website. This engagement drive signals back to Google, which in turn pushes us up the search rankings. I know of at least one very major project we have won because of the awareness this created – and the ROI for this work is at least 10,000 per cent.

Pragmatic curiosity

This section is a practical hands-on guide to using digital channels in the real world in a time-efficient way. However, it is also essential that we don't ignore potential options because of untested assumptions and that we don't become afraid of the new.

Digital marketing is generally moving at an incredible pace, and this is not going to slow down. It is very easy, and often sensible, to be suspicious of the never-ending flow of new channels and to adopt an 'I'll use it when it's been proven' approach. We do need to commit, however, to trying things out, albeit in a pragmatic and sensible fashion. In this section we explore how this is possible in practice.

Latest tools and techniques

Let's face it, by the time you read this there will be lots of new stuff that has happened between the time of writing and the book going to print. For that reason, I will be filtering and highlighting on the website that accompanies this book. I would also love your feedback and I'm happy to publicize your efforts and experiences:
http://www.targetinternet.com/digitalbranding

Social media

Social media has had the greatest impact on branding of any of the digital 'channels' we discuss in this section. Actually, calling social media a channel doesn't put it in perspective properly. Social media has fundamentally changed how we engage and interact with brands and has led to the fundamental shift in branding that this book is all about.

The fundamental shift is to that of two-way communications and empowerment of the consumer (in both B2C and B2B contexts). All of the topics we have discussed up until now, including the need for authenticity, clear value proposition and the increased complexity of the user journey, are all because of social media.

Through social media, rather than just broadcasting *at* you, I can engage *with* you. If you take any of the traditional branding metrics such as awareness and recall – brand awareness is the extent to which a brand is recognized by potential customers; brand recall is when a brand is correctly associated with a particular product, branding or characteristic – they are far more likely to be impacted by 'engaging with' than they are by just 'looking at' something. However, engagement takes effort, so you first need to provide value in order to get them to engage. That value may take many forms, from entertaining through to educating (and potentially both at the same time), but you must give them an incentive to engage.

Social is personal

What we need to consider is how to best utilize this social behaviour for our organizations and to help achieve our business objectives, while providing value and without interrupting an individual's private and personal space. Over 76 per cent of Facebook users are at least 'slightly concerned' about privacy issues (Statista, 2013), which indicates a general awareness of how all the data that we share via social media carries some risks.

User journey and value proposition

Two of the main themes that we discussed in Part One were understanding the user journey and considering our value proposition. These considerations are key to using social media effectively. We need to make sure that we understand which social platforms our target audience is using and make sure that when they use these platforms the user experience provides value. Too much social media activity is carried out just for the sake of activity.

Content and engagement

Our ability to utilize social media effectively will come down to having interesting and useful content to share, and being willing and able to engage in an open and authentic way. Because of the personal nature of social media, a standard 'corporate communications' tone doesn't work. Even in a B2B environment, we are still dealing with individuals and need to apply core social media principles to our communications.

Bear in mind that anyone can blog, post to social media sites and tweet. In fact, many best practice guides say that for maximum impact you should tweet around four times per day (Adobe, 2013). You should only do this, though, if you have something interesting to say.

Mobile social media experience

We need to consider the fact that the majority of people using social media on mobile devices are using apps to access these platforms.

I personally use the Facebook, Twitter, Google+ and LinkedIn apps on my iPhone every day. So what does this particular way of accessing social media mean in terms of our mobile marketing? It means that we need to think in terms of accessing our content via the constraints of these apps.

For example, if you post content to Twitter (or Weibo sites in China), most of the time you will be sharing a link. How does that link display on a mobile device? With over 60 per cent of Twitter users accessing the service via mobile device (Marketing Land, 2013), we need to consider the mobile experience of the links we are driving people through to. My own tweets split into two core categories: linking to useful content on my site and linking to useful content on other people's sites. I know that the experience on my site has been fully optimized for mobile users, but is this the case for other sites I am driving people through to?

Another example is using social networks such as Facebook and LinkedIn. Generally in this case we are posting content to try and create engagement, and very often this content will include images. The images may display very well on a desktop-size screen, but how do they look on a mobile? Much of the social network experience is different in a mobile app as opposed to a desktop version. We need to make sure we have considered this in all of our social posts. We have to assume that users will be on a mobile device at some point and therefore make sure that everything works in this format.

Informing your social media approach

Before we start any social media activity we need to start by listening. We need to understand what our audience is interested in and passionate about in order to inform our approach in providing value. In fact, social listening can help inform our digital branding overall, not just the social elements. There is a wide range of 'listening' or 'monitoring' tools, which will be discussed below. Understanding how someone searches can help inform our understanding of what their needs and interests are.

Using search to inform content themes

Google Trends is a fantastic free tool that allows us to see how users search in Google – and the trends that show over time. The great thing about this tool is that not only can we understand search trends but we can use this to inform our social content. We look at this tool in more detail in Chapter 6 (Search) and again when we look at judging the impact of our digital branding efforts (Chapter 12: Measuring digital branding), but here we use it to find out what people are interested in, in order to inform what we should be talking about on our social platforms.

In the screen shot shown in Figure 5.1, looking at the word 'jobs' we can start to see a clear seasonal trend. The peak in searches every year is in January, when many of us have new year resolutions and decide to look for a new job. This tapers off as we get back to work, and then many of us go on our summer vacation and get fired up again about looking for a new job. We then realize that Christmas is just around the corner and think we'll leave it to the new year. And this pattern carries on year after year! In the last four years, due to the global financial crisis, more people have been looking for jobs and therefore searching. Finally, we can see a huge increase in searches for 'jobs' in October 2011. Why? Because Steve Jobs (former CEO of

FIGURE 5.1   Google Trends allows us to see volumes of searches for a particular phrase over time. This chart shows searches for the word 'jobs', **http://www.google.co.uk/trends**

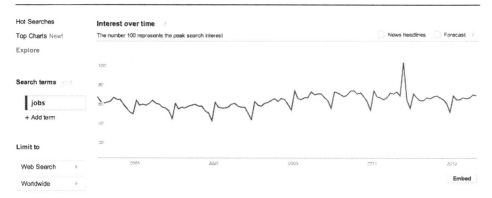

(Google and the Google logo are registered trademarks of Google Inc, used with permission)

Apple) died, and it creates a skew in our results because of the amount of people searching for his surname.

The Google Trends tool, as standard, will show you relative search volume over time for a particular word or phrase. We can drill down by time region, country or language. The tool tries to identify related news stories at points on the graph, and shows us geographical interest and the most popular and fastest rising variations of these search terms. Probably the most important feature is the ability to compare the trends for different search terms, and this is particularly important for informing content.

Figure 5.2 shows the phrases 'internet marketing' and 'digital marketing' being compared. We can see a decline in interest for internet

FIGURE 5.2   Comparing words in Google Trends

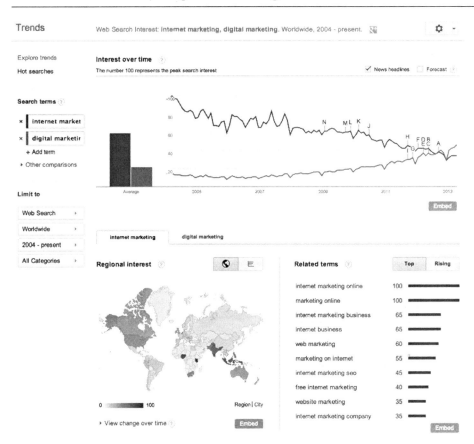

(Google and the Google logo are registered trademarks of Google Inc, used with permission)

marketing and a rise in interest for digital marketing. I clearly need to be talking about digital marketing rather than internet marketing on my social platform, because that's what people are searching for and are interested in.

One thing to be clear on is that Google Trends shows you relative volumes of searches, not the actual numbers of searches. If you want the actual number of searches, you'll need to use the keyword planner (we discuss this in Chapter 6). Relative volume will show a word at a score of 100 at its highest volume of searches and the rest of the score is relative to this. When multiple words are compared, the highest point given a 100 score is the most searched of the words being compared at its highest search volume.

One of the limitations of the Google Trends tool is its lack of ability to show trends for niche search terms. You'll find in many cases that a niche search term shows that it doesn't have enough data to plot a chart.

Social listening tools

Social listening tools are something that every organization of every size should be using. They allow you to monitor a number of different social channels to look for activity around certain phrases or topics. This capability can be used at a number of stages throughout social media campaigns and they are an essential tool for effective social media use.

First, these tools can be used in the 'listening' stage, when you are trying to understand what social channels your audience is using, what they are saying, what they are interested in and what your competitors are doing. Many organizations will carry out a listening project before starting any social media activity, as part of their standard process before initiating a campaign.

Second, these tools can be used to monitor the effectiveness of our social media activity. We can monitor groups of words and phrases to see what is happening on an ongoing basis, and how our audience reacts to our social activity.

Finally, social listening tools can be used to manage outreach and engagement, by identifying key influencers on social channels. This can be important when trying to grow your audience, but also when dealing with negative feedback or a crisis. The idea is to influence the influencers, much like in traditional PR, but in the case of social media we can do this at a much more granular level.

Some social listening tools also include elements of workflow management, and help you to manage your social media efforts. For example, you may be able to track which social media users you have engaged with, which individual in your organization was involved, and plan future activities.

Social media monitoring and listening tools

There is a huge array of social media monitoring tools out there, varying wildly in price and capability. At the free end of the spectrum you'll find a wide variety of tools. However these tools are fairly limited, and the old adage that you get what you pay for generally holds true. It's worth checking out SocialMention.com and Addictomatic.com (not really a social listening tool, but it can be helpful) for examples of what you can get.

The amount of paid tools available is dizzying, but I would certainly recommend the following:

- **http://www.viralheat.com** – low cost and practical social monitoring. I use this one daily.

- **http://www.brandwatch.com** – my favourite social monitoring tool and well worth the cost. Very powerful, flexible and used by some of the world's leading companies.

- **http://www.sproutsocial.com** – another great tool at a reasonable cost with some great management features.

- **http://www.salesforcemarketingcloud.com** – Radian6 is owned by SalesForce, the cloud base CRM platform. Powerful and suited to very large brands due to its pricing.

You can find a list of even more tools on our website:
http://www.targetinternet.com/digitalbranding

Social analysis tools

Social analysis tools are different to social listening/monitoring tools in that they generally look at one social platform and give some analysis or functionality for that particular platform. In fact, many social media sites have these built in. For example, Facebook Insights will give you a range of reports that allow you to see which of your posts were most popular, where the users that like you are in the world, and who is engaging with your content.

There are literally thousands of these tools out there. Generally they will analyse your audience and content and provide some insight into how to take your campaigns forward. I have highlighted a couple below to give a flavour of what you can expect:

- **http://www.tweriod.com** – find out the most effective time of day and day of the week to post your tweets.

- **http://twtrland.com** – analyse your Twitter audience with this excellent free tool (see Figure 5.3).

- Facebook Insights – accessed when you have set up a Facebook page, this lets you know what content is working.

- YouTube Insights – accessed via the social platform itself, it lets you find out which of your videos are actually getting engagement.

- **http://www.followerwonk.com** – an oddly named but very powerful tool for analysing Twitter audiences and growing your audience, part of the moz.com set of tools.

The list could go on and on, so we've compiled and are constantly updating a huge list on the website to accompany this book: **http://www.targetinternet.com/digitalbranding**

Social media in China

If you are targeting the huge potential of the Chinese market, or are working within China, you need to be aware (or probably already are) that social media in China can, on first sight, look very different to elsewhere in the world. Actually, the core principles of content, engagement and transparency all still apply, but you will find yourself using completely different platforms.

In most countries globally the social media platforms are fairly universal (with a few exceptions such as Mixi in Japan or VK in Russia), but in China there is no Twitter, Facebook or YouTube. Instead there are local market equivalents. RenRen and PengYou are social networks similar to Facebook. Weibos are microblogs like Twitter and there are several, including Sina Weibo and Tencent Weibo. QQ is the most popular instant messenger and Youku is a popular equivalent to YouTube.

Just like any market, you need to understand what social platforms your target audience is using and then engage using the right tone and content.

For a great resource on social media in China, and the whole Asia region, take a look at: **http://www.techinasia.com**

FIGURE 5.3   An example of the many social analysis tools out there and one of my favourites, twtrland.com analyses my Twitter account

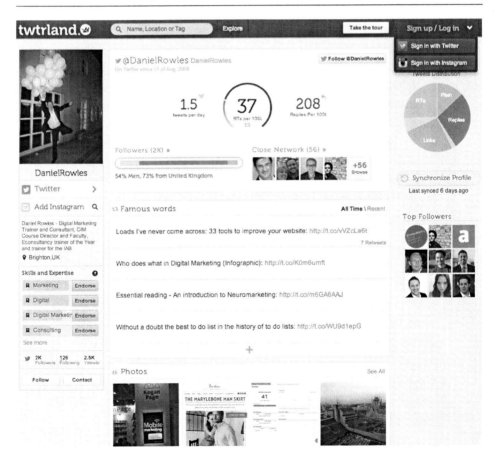

Analytics

Your web analytics is one of the most powerful tools for informing your social media activity. You'll not only be able to understand which social media sites are driving traffic to your website, but also how many of these visitors are on mobile devices – and on which devices.

We'll explore analytics in more detail in Part Three, but it is worth mentioning at this point that analytics can help you understand the impact of your social media campaigns on your broader digital objectives.

The importance of Google Analytics

Google Analytics is a powerful and sophisticated web analytics platform that also happens to be free. It has around 82 per cent market share of the entire analytics market (Techcrunch, 2013) and is improving and offering more and more functionality all the time. It is suitable for the majority of site owners' needs and offers extensive reports around mobile sites and apps.

There are, of course, other commercial analytics packages available, and these have the advantage of account managers and service level agreements. Google Analytics Premium does offer these things, but pricing is currently US $150,000 per year.

Real-world integration

One of the greatest opportunities with any digital branding is to integrate multiple channels together and work throughout each stage of the user journey. Social media gives us the opportunity to tie together online and offline experiences and merge them into more seamless experiences. We explore this idea in detail in Chapter 11 (From integration to transmedia campaigns).

Policy and planning

You have worked out the kind of content you need and you understand which channels are appropriate for your target audience. You have also thought through the user experience and made sure that it is optimized at each stage of your digital branding. So, are you ready to start your social media activity? No, not quite. One of the most important elements of successful social media is having a clear and workable social media policy and set of guidelines.

Social media policies are there to help anyone involved in carrying out your social activity and to outline the dos and don'ts of social media within your organization. They help you to use social media in an effective way, keep you focused on providing value, avoid social media disasters and generally make social media an effective part of your digital branding.

A social media policy will outline things such as:

- the reporting structure of the team involved with social media and clear direction on where to seek advice;
- appropriate social media channels;
- guidance on tone of voice;
- guidance on suggested tools, log ins and who should be using them;
- the process for identification and mitigation of risks;
- escalation policy for use when problems are identified;
- responsibilities and legal requirements;
- guidance on suitable content;
- direction on frequency of content posting;
- moderation guidelines;
- best practice on posting mobile-optimized content;
- guidance on creating mobile-optimized landing pages;
- mobile testing platforms;
- guide to success measures and relevant analytics reports.

Every organization should have its own social media policy that can help mitigate risks, create effective and consistent social communications and make sure that everyone understands how this will impact your digital branding.

Database of social media policies

This site has a huge list of example social media policies that you can review and get insights from for your own.

At the time of publishing there were nearly 250 policies listed:

http://socialmediagovernance.com/policies.php

The social media benchmark and social policy

The Chartered Institute of Marketing has been running an initiative called the Social Media Benchmark for some time and, in June 2013, they published the third iteration of the study. Up until this version they had focused on understanding how organizations have been using social media and how well managed it was.

The general results had been that we were all using more social media and we really didn't have a strategy as to why! Worrying, but certainly not surprising in my opinion. As time went on, the need for a social strategy seemed to be more apparent to people, and things seemed to be gradually improving.

Then came wave three of the benchmark. I was lucky enough to be speaking at the first CIM Digital Summit at Bloomberg TV and was honoured to be doing the keynote speech. Thomas Brown, Associate Director of Research and Insights at the CIM, was planning on releasing the data at the event. He had agreed, however, that we could do a sneak preview of the data on the digital marketing podcast that I run. When I read the results I nearly fell off my seat: over 60 per cent of organizations had no process in place to deal with the risks of social media.

Policy and the risk to digital branding

This third iteration of the benchmark had focused on risk mitigation in social media, the idea being that we had all realized by now that social media offers a fantastic set of opportunities, but it also comes with plenty of risk, as shown by the constant flow of social media disasters. The questions were all focused on how many people had social media policies, how good they were and how much they were being used.

The responses were fairly worrying. Most people saw the risk in social media but the majority of organizations had no social media policy in place and those that did hadn't really adopted it – or it wasn't appropriate for the job in regard to level of detail. Figure 5.4 shows the core findings in an infographic from the study here.

Fundamentally, this is a critical risk to digital branding. The effective and risk-mitigated use of social media is intrinsic to what we are talking about throughout this book. This risk mitigation is not just an exercise in corporate governance, but a signal of how important we realize this channel is, and an indicator of the high regard with which we hold our customer communications and engagement. This study basically told us that the majority of organizations still don't get it.

Outreach, engagement and ego

To really get the most from our digital branding, we should always consider how we can maximize our reach into our target audience. Social outreach and engagement is a highly effective way of doing this, and as well as increasing the size of our audience it can help us to create positive engagement.

If I keep on publishing useful and engaging content, regularly update my social channels and positively engage with anyone who leaves comments or feedback, I will gradually grow my social media audience. If, however, I want to speed up this process and create the maximum amplification for my efforts then I am going to need to focus on social media outreach.

Social media outreach is all about identifying the key influencers and advocates within a particular group. If I can get these key people

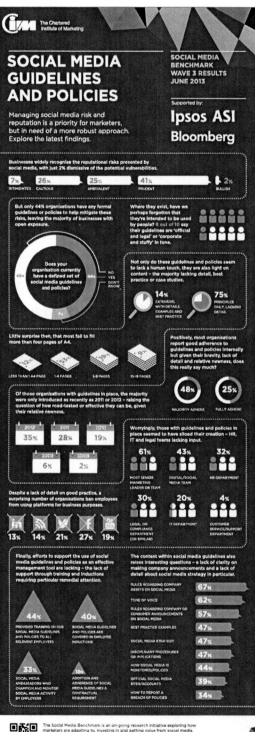

FIGURE 5.4
The infographic for the Chartered Institute of Marketing's Social Media Benchmark wave 3

to share my updates and content then I can amplify my visibility and potentially grow my audience.

So let's define what we mean by an influencer or an advocate.

Advocates are the easiest group to identify as they are those people who leave positive comments, re-tweet things and generally engage in a positive way. They are willing to spread what you say and add to your social voice. They are our greatest asset and we need to engage, encourage and reward this group in order to build loyalty.

Influencers are those people with access to the audience that we want to influence. We can use social media tools to identify them and we then need a strategy to get engagement and encourage them to become advocates.

Judging influence

You can use a number of measures to judge influence online. You could look at the number of social connections that someone has, or look at the quality of their audience. You could consider how likely it is that what they say will be read and repeated. This process can be quite time-consuming and therefore it is worth considering some of the key tools that can help us understand influence.

Klout, shown in Figure 5.5, aims to take the pain away from trying to work out influence online. It works by looking at a range of social

FIGURE 5.5   Klout is a social media influence scoring platform

platforms, assessing over 400 different factors, such as your likelihood of being re-tweeted, and then gives you a score out of 100. It will also assign topics that it believes you are influential about. In the screenshot in Figure 5.5 I currently have a score of 62 and, according to Klout, I am influential about social media, mobile marketing and digital marketing (phew!).

Scoring services such as Klout have actually received a lot of negative press and have been accused of everything from being inaccurate through to being nothing more than a way of flattering people's egos. I disagree. Although Klout is far from perfect, as their algorithm (the set of rules behind the scores) improves, so does its effectiveness. There will always be arguments about how much a particular factor or platform should be weighted, but in reality it can give you the rough guidance you need. If I look at all of my Twitter followers and look at those with the highest Klout scores, there is no doubt that these people are my most influential audience.

The key point of Klout is that it provides a nice easy metric to initially assess influence – you can then dig a little deeper and plan your outreach campaigns. For example, I have a plug-in for Google Chrome that shows me the Klout score of all the people whose tweets I am reading on Twitter. That way I can see who is most influential and can prioritize my engagement activities accordingly.

There are other social influence tools out there, and you may also want to take a look at **http://www.kred.com** and some of the Twitter analysis tools that we have already mentioned, which can be useful for this as well.

Another approach to judging social influence is to use a social monitoring tool that helps you to identify the most influential users on a particular platform. The screenshot in Figure 5.6 is taken from the ViralHeat social media listening tool that we mentioned earlier in this chapter. It shows two groups of potentially influential users on the topic of 'SEO', showing those people who have tweeted the most on this topic in the last seven days and those people who have tweeted about SEO but also have the most followers. I can then reach out to these people and find a way to engage with them and build some form of relationship.

FIGURE 5.6 Using ViralHeat.com to identify influential Twitter users on the topic of SEO

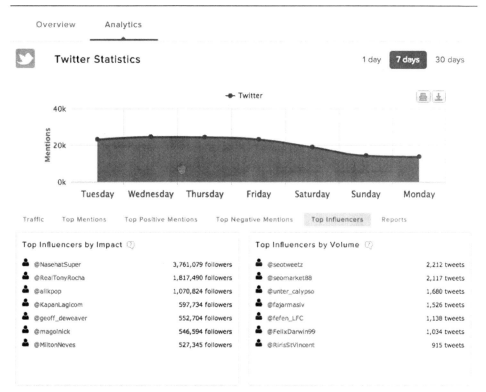

Brand, social media, online PR and search optimization

It is important to understand that there is a very close connection between your social media activity, Public Relations (PR) activity and search optimization. It is also essential to realize that all of these things make up a significant part of your digital branding. We will look at search in more detail in the next chapter, but the effectiveness of your social media activity will create 'social signals' that influence your search rankings (essential to the quantity and quality of conversation that is happening in social media around your topics of interest).

Social engagement and outreach are essentially online PR, but your offline PR activities can also impact what you talk about in social media and how many people are linking to your sites and social media platforms. For this reason, we need everyone involved in these three disciplines to be working collaboratively and be aware of what each other are doing.

Social measurement

The greatest mistake made in a huge number of organizations (in my experience the majority) is to focus on volume-based metrics when looking at social media campaigns. More often than not, a campaign is started and the initial target is to reach a certain number of likes or followers. But, in reality, what does having a million followers actually mean? The answer is actually very little. We need to understand who that audience is, look at how engaged they are, their sentiment and, most importantly, understand if social media is actually having an impact on your business objectives.

Part Three looks at analytics and measurement in much more detail, but we can use analytics in a number of ways to look at the success of our social media effects. We can start with the basics and look at how much traffic we get from social media sites to our websites. We could then take it a stage further and look at how many of these visits are on mobile devices. If you are using analytics effectively, you also will have set up goals, and you can see what part social media is having on driving your website visitors to complete your goals. All of this will be covered in more detail in Part Three, but the key point to remember here is that it's not just about the social media data, such as number of followers or amount of engagement, it is actually about understanding how this drives your end objectives.

Sentiment analysis

Many social media tools will carry out some form of sentiment analysis. The idea is that the context of the social media mentions that you receive is analysed, and the sentiment or intention of the social media user is understood. This most usually takes the form of grouping these mentions into positive, negative and neutral.

There is a problem, however. The majority of social media tools get this completely wrong. These tools work by analysing the text and using fairly rudimentary methods of analysing the language. For example, if I tweet 'Top 10 digital marketing disasters of 2014' and then link to my website, many tools will see this as a negative tweet and associate negativity with the link to my website. It will be seen as negative due to the use of the word 'disaster', even though from experience I know that this will actually be a very popular tweet. Some tools, however, are a lot more effective at analysing language and take a far more sophisticated approach. These tools certainly aren't 100 per cent accurate, but they are far less likely to make rudimentary mistakes like this.

The solution is to understand how effective your particular tool is at analysing the social platforms you are looking at, and then manually checking the results you get. This doesn't mean reading every single tweet or comment (although in an ideal world you will), but it certainly means scanning through and understanding the assumption that the tool is making.

This is particularly important when you look at 'share of voice' (a measure that we look at in detail in Part Three). During a really bad social media crisis, when everyone is talking about you and saying negative things, your share of voice will be high. You therefore need to understand sentiment when you look at share of voice.

Social media advertising

Many social media platforms give you a number of paid advertising options. Major search engines such as Google, Yandex and Baidu also allow you to run paid search campaigns (discussed in more depth in Chapter 6). We need to discuss the implications of paid social campaigns here, however, as they can heavily impact the effectiveness and measurement of your social campaigns.

Value proposition, privacy and trust

Since social media is very much part of our personal lives in many cases, we need to be very cautious about how we use it in a commercial way. Almost everything we have spoken about so far involves providing value via engagement and understanding the user's needs. Exactly the same principle should be applied to social media advertising.

We need to consider how much of an interruption social advertising can actually be seen as, how it can actually damage our brands if used badly and what image of our organization we are projecting. Facebook is responding to this, and already there are signs that users will be able to opt out of most ads on mobile devices if they wish to (Atlantic Wire, 2013).

The key point is to understand the social platforms you are using, why a user is there and to make sure that the value proposition is clear. If you are on Facebook and you are interested in health and fitness, and a brand such as Nike offers you free tools to help you achieve your fitness goals, then that's great. If, however, you are on Facebook and you have liked a digital marketing podcast, it doesn't mean that any of your friends necessarily have an interest (see Figure 5.7).

The screenshot in Figure 5.7 shows how much of an impact running a promotion on a post in Facebook can boost your audience. In this particular case, the sharp rise in audience and engagement, shown by the steep rise in the chart, was caused by 'boosting' a post. Boosting a post is basically promoting it to your audience. Promoting posts will make your post more visible to those people who have already liked you, but it also means that your post is shown to the friends

FIGURE 5.7   Facebook Insights showing the impact of promoting a post on audience size

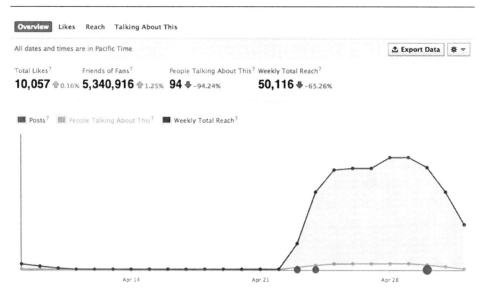

of your likes as well. Although, in this particular case, this led to an increase in overall likes and engagement (as well as a knock-on impact in Klout score), what isn't clear is how many people saw the ad who it wasn't relevant for, and how much of an impact this had on what these people thought of my brand. The problem is that there is no way of finding out who these people are and what impact these ads have had on them or their perception of my brand.

Trusting algorithms

It is actually in Facebook's interest not to annoy people with irrelevant ads, just as it is not good for Google to give you irrelevant search results. Both scenarios lead to dissatisfied users, which in turn leads to those users moving to other social networks and search engines. The problem is that Facebook is under serious pressure (Telegraph, 2013) to increase its profits but it can't do this at the expense of losing users.

The algorithms – which are just sets of rules and logic – behind these sites are what decide on what ads you are shown or what search results you are given. Google has spent many years and much investment in developing its algorithms and focusing on relevancy. For Facebook it is relatively early days, and mobile advertising for Facebook is something that has existed for less than a year. As time goes on, the algorithm that targets the advertising is likely to become more advanced and more effective at doing this in a highly targeted way.

Social media conclusions

As well as needing to consider all of the usual complexities of social media when planning our digital branding, we have some additional things to take into account. We still need to consider appropriate use of channels, focus on content and engagement, and find effective measurement strategies. Most importantly with digital branding, we need to consider the overall user experience and be very clearly focused on transparency and trust.

The overall user experience is all down to making sure we have thought through and tested how the user will actually experience our social media content and how they can engage with us. Although time-consuming and fragmented, due to the number of social platforms and scenarios involved, it is a very practical and reasonably straightforward issue.

Trust, on the other hand, is far more subjective but is of huge importance. Social media can act as a magnifier for missteps we make as marketers. By interrupting, being irrelevant or making incorrect assumptions we will actually inconvenience our target audience. This may be by giving them irrelevant content to scroll past, or bombarding them with the same message again and again.

Social media is at the heart of what makes digital branding so special – and it carries both risk and opportunity. A well-planned and strategic approach to social media will not only make best use of the tools and channels available, but will do so with a view on how this makes up part of the broader user journey.

CASE STUDY   HSBC

Background

HSBC Expat provides financial services for people living and working abroad. For many, arranging expat finances, if it is considered at all, is less urgent than finding accommodation, a job and schools.

Objectives

HSBC's objective was to engage with expats earlier in the research process, establishing it as a trusted source of information about the process of moving abroad. They wanted to create useful online content about life abroad as the first step in establishing a relationship with expats and providing opportunities to talk about their expat products and services via their website.

Their main aim was to create awareness of HSBC Expat, engage with expats and convert them into customers. They aimed to reach 20,000 users in 50 countries in the first three months.

Strategy and execution

HSBC Expat decided to create engaging content about topics important to expats. They harnessed HSBC's stakeholders – customers, employees, corporate and media – to create 'informal' tips on expat life: a cost-effective way to create relevant and reusable content. The goal of this content-marketing approach was to attract expats through social and search, engage them with useful content, then drive them to the main website.

HSBC developed a microsite, 'Expat Hints and Tips'. The concept is based on motivations for sharing: expats share tips to help other expats, to demonstrate their knowledge or both (see Figure 5.8).

They coordinated owned, earned and paid media activity – eg the most popular 'Top 5' lists became calls to action for paid media, achieving higher click-through rates (CTRs) and engagement due to the relevance of the content. They used web and social media analytics 'big data', extracting over 1 billion data points into bespoke tableau dashboards for analysis. They also conducted post-launch usability testing with expats.

Results

The site has been used by expats all over the world. This increased awareness has helped contribute to increased brand term searches for HSBC Expat, with search traffic up 30.92 per cent and leads up 52.14 per cent.

The launch and associated tweets helped their Twitter channel (@expatexplorer) to become HSBC's second most followed globally, with over 12,000 followers.

FIGURE 5.8   Expats share tips to help other expats, to demonstrate their knowledge or both

FIGURE 5.9   Twitter recently accounted for 47 per cent of the respondents sourced by HSBC Marketing for HSBC's annual Expat Explorer survey

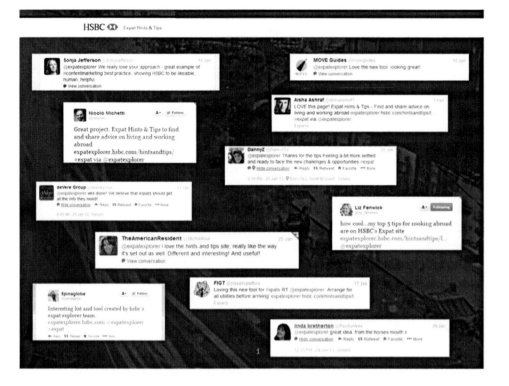

The **57** per cent growth in followers post-launch makes Twitter a more valuable channel for them. Twitter recently accounted for 47 per cent of the respondents sourced by HSBC Marketing for HSBC's annual Expat Explorer survey, outperforming other channels for the first time (see Figure 5.9).

Q&A: Richard Fray, Manager, Digital Experience, HSBC Expat

What was the insight that underpinned your strategy and tactics?
HSBC's research found that the uncertainties of a move abroad can be overwhelming: 'Exciting, lonely, frustrating, eye-opening, rewarding, fun, isolating, maddening' (Respondent, HSBC's Expat Explorer Survey).

Focus groups told us that alongside HSBC's country, tax and finance guides, expats wanted 'informal' advice from other expats, like that on forums. They felt this fit with HSBC's international brand.

Research by the *New York Times* ('Why Do People Share Online?') found that two major motivations for sharing content online are: 1) to bring valuable content to others; 2) to define ourselves to others.

Expats fit this model. Those that have moved abroad have experiences that they are happy to share on blogs and forums, both to help those about to follow in their footsteps and to establish themselves as experienced expats.

What metrics did you put in place to track the effectiveness of your solution?
We used web and social media analytics 'big data', extracting over 1 billion data points into bespoke tableau dashboards for analysis. We also conducted post-launch usability testing with expats.

Key performance indicators:

- Awareness:
  - unique visits;
  - visitor location;
  - social media reach.

- Engagement:
  - number of tips submitted;
  - social shares;
  - Twitter followers;
  - social media comments;
  - usability testing results.

- Conversion:
  - leads generated by users of the site and through search.

What were the biggest challenges you faced while developing this campaign?
The two biggest challenges were, first, how to attribute business results such as leads generated to activity that was very much aimed at the top of the sales funnel for generating awareness. Typically we are engaging people who may be months away from moving abroad and at a very early stage in the planning process, and potentially not thinking about the financial aspects of their move yet, which is itself a complex purchase. We needed to be able to identify whether these users of the Hints and Tips site eventually generated a lead, even months later, rather than purely applying, say, a 'last click' model for this (see Figure 5.10). In addition we needed to consider and value secondary benefits such as improved SEO [search engine optimization], reuseable content, improved engagement. Andrew Hood at Lynchpin helped us with this analysis, as well as creating an animated heatmap so that we could see the viral spread of the site around the world.

FIGURE 5.10   Expat Hints and Tips reached 174 countries in two months

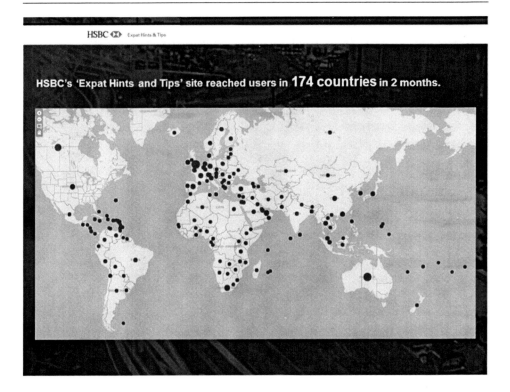

The second and related challenge was 'what happens next?' – how to sensitively and elegantly encourage users of the Hints and Tips site to begin exploring other aspects of our offering. The ultimate goal was for these users to open an account with us, if that met their needs, but the transition from light, engaging and interesting content to product information and a sales conversation is a delicate one. We sought to address this by providing contextual, relevant links to other useful information on our website that sought to nudge users deeper into the sales funnel without turning them off with aggressive product push. We acknowledge that there is more work for us to do here and we are continually testing and refining this part of the customer journey.

Search

Search is a fundamental part of the user journey. What we search for – and the results that we find – have a massive impact on our digital branding. Making sure we understand what our target audience is searching for at different stages of the user journey will be essential in order to deliver the best user experience. If we can't be found, or if we drive our audience through to a poor user experience, we will damage our digital branding. The best website in the world is useless if it can't be found.

We would normally divide search into two key areas: 1) natural (or organic) search, the area of the search results decided upon by the search engines; 2) paid search, the set of results that we can pay to be visible in. Search engine optimization (SEO) is the process of achieving search rankings within the natural/organic results. Pay per click (PPC) refers to the paid search element of search results. We explore both in this chapter.

Let's start by giving an example of how search tools can demonstrate the importance of search as part of our digital branding. Figures 6.1 and 6.2 are screenshots from Google Trends, a fantastic tool that we explore more later in this chapter. These two screenshots show the reaction to a TV campaign in regard to users doing search.

Enter the drumming gorilla

Back in 2006, a lifetime ago in digital marketing terms, Cadbury, the confectionery manufacturer, released a viral TV campaign. This involved a very intense scene of a gorilla listening to music and then playing the drums along to the music. The music in question was 'In the Air Tonight' by Phil Collins, and if you haven't seen this ad then go and search for 'drumming gorilla ad' on YouTube.

FIGURE 6.1　Searches in Google for 'drumming gorilla'

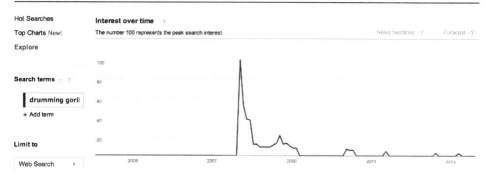

(Google and the Google logo are registered trademarks of Google Inc, used with permission)

FIGURE 6.2　Searches in Google for 'drumming gorilla' and 'Cadbury'

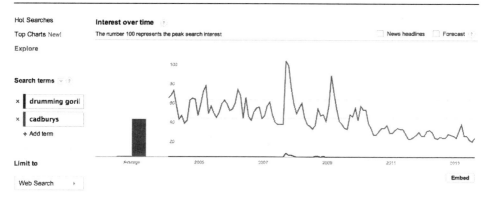

(Google and the Google logo are registered trademarks of Google Inc, used with permission)

This was the first ad of its type and it caused a huge amount of conversation, mainly because people had no idea what a gorilla playing the drums had to do with Cadbury's chocolate. The answer is very little, but this randomness was the campaign's genius. So what did people do when they saw the ad? They did a search on Google.

Figure 6.1 shows that there were no searches for drumming gorillas on Google until the ad came out (not all that surprising), but when it did there was a spike in searches for this term.

However, what Figure 6.2 shows is that what people actually searched for is 'Cadburys', meaning that the brand experience was going to be massively impacted by search. This shows that we need to anticipate the target audience's reaction to every channel that we use and realize that even traditional broadcast channels are now impacted massively by our digital branding.

SEM – my least favourite three-letter acronym

As you have probably already worked out, we love three-letter acronyms in digital marketing. Of all these acronyms, SEM is my least favourite. It stands for search engine marketing, and technically speaking (I'll happily argue until I'm blue in the face over this) it means both sides of search marketing – that is, both SEO and PPC. However, it is often used to describe the paid side of search, PPC.

In reality, we could place PPC in the advertising section of this book, because that's exactly what it is, a form of paid advertising. However, the term *online advertising* is most often used to refer to banner and video ads, so for the sake of consistency with this definition, we'll discuss PPC within this section of the book.

The PPC/SEO relationship

There has always been discussion and rumour around how much your SEO results are boosted by spending money on PPC campaigns. The answer, for the vast majority of search engines, including Google, is that there is no direct correlation whatsoever. I have had clients spending millions of pounds every month, and there was no direct impact on their natural search rankings. This rule, however, doesn't follow for Baidu, the largest search engine in China. Fundamentally, the more you are spending with Baidu, the better your natural search visibility tends to be. It's a nice easy way to get search rankings, but probably not the best way to give the user the most relevant search results.

Search engine optimization

SEO is all about getting to the top of the search engine results in the organic results. Thankfully, the core rules of SEO are consistent across all major search engines and we will explore those core concepts here. We also look at how the user journey impacts search and what we need in order to maximize its positive impact on our digital branding.

It all starts with spiders

Spiders are bits of software that read your pages and send the content back to the search engines. If they can't read your site, you won't get rankings.

The search engine spiders (also known as bots or robots) visit your website, follow the links on your pages and send your content back to the search engine so it can then be assessed and ranked. This data that has been sent back to the search engines and has been assessed is known as the search engine index. Generally, the more often you update your content, and the more important your website is seen to be (we'll cover this 'importance' later in the chapter when we look at link building), the more often the spiders will come back to look at your content.

There are certain practices that can stop the spiders from reading your content in the first place and, clearly, if your website can't be read, you won't get ranked. A good example of this is building your entire site in Flash. Flash is a proprietary technology from Adobe that allows you to build animated and interactive web content. Google and the other search engines find it difficult, or choose not to read the content inside Flash. This basically means that the search engine sees the 'box' that contains the content, rather than the content itself. You should also remember that Flash will not work on an iOS device (iPhones and iPads). Flash has been used by agencies for many years to create 'rich' and 'brand focused' websites – this basically translates as using the web channel inappropriately to create something over-animated. If you need to create anything interactive and animated, use HTML5. It's better for the search engines and works on more mobile devices.

Mobile search

Mobile search is growing phenomenally, with both Google and Baidu reporting over 1,000 per cent growth in search on mobile devices in the past three years (SearchEngineLand, 2013). With more and more users relying on mobile searches, and evidence showing that around 73 per cent of mobile searches end in an action (Researchscape, 2013), mobile search is an essential part of any mobile strategy.

Desktop versus mobile results

The major search engines, and particularly Google, will try to give a mobile-optimized search experience. This means you will be given different search results depending on the device you search on. It also means that because of this optimization, which may include things such as local results shown on a map, given the limited screen space available on mobile devices it becomes even more important to come as near the top of the results as possible (see Figure 6.3).

Google and some of the other search engines' spiders will attempt to visit your site and act as a mobile device to look for a mobile-optimized experience (Google, 2013). Sites that are offering an improved mobile experience are then given a boost within the search rankings. This evidence is somewhat subjective, however, as the spiders can detect a difference between desktop and mobile sites, but cannot determine whether it is an optimal experience.

FIGURE 6.3 Mobile search results when looking for a location-specific term

(Google and the Google logo are registered trademarks of Google Inc, used with permission)

Google operators

If you want to check that Google is visiting your website and when the spiders last visited, you can use the following technique, known as a Google operator. Go to Google as normal, but instead of searching for a word or phrase, type the following into the search box: cache:www.yourwebsite.com.

This will bring back a copy of your website and some details that tell you when Google last visited your site. If this returns nothing it may mean that Google is not visiting your website.

Google webmaster tools

For some real insight into how Google's spiders are accessing your pages and any problems they may be having, you need to install Google Webmaster Tools. You can find Google Webmaster Tools here: **http://www.google.com/webmasters/tools**

You'll need a Google account to set things up (you can set one up in a couple of minutes) and you'll then need to prove that you own the website you want to get some details on. Google provides step-by-step instructions, but you will need to be able to either edit your web page's code or to create a new page with a specific name (as this demonstrates to Google that you control the website).

Once installed, Google Webmaster Tools allows you to do the following:

- **Get Google's view of your site and diagnose problems:** you can see how Google crawls and indexes your site and learn about specific problems they're having in accessing it – probably the most important feature in regard to what we have been talking about.

- **Discover your link and query traffic:** you can view and download data about internal and external links to your site with the link reporting tools, find out which Google search words/phrases drive traffic to your site, and see exactly how users arrive there.

- **Share information about your site:** this allows you to tell Google about your pages with Sitemaps, which pages are the most important to you and how often they change.

It also has some features that allow you to see how fast your pages load in comparison to other sites. This is important as it is one of the factors that Google considers when deciding your rankings.

Keyword research for SEO

Keyword research is all about understanding how our potential audience searches so that we know what search phrases we need to rank for. Once we've done this we need to look at getting the words onto our pages (we'll cover this below when we discuss on-page optimization).

It is too easy to make assumptions about what words and phrases our potential audience is searching for, based on our own opinions (or possibly the opinions of our search agency). We need to back this up with real facts, and happily there are plenty of free tools that allow us to do just this.

Keyword challenges

Some of the everyday challenges you will face in keyword research are best demonstrated by giving an example. When I ran a search agency we had a large recruitment client whose basic brief was: 'We want to be number one for the word "jobs".' What they were basically asking for was to be number one out of about 3.6 billion pages (just search for a phrase in Google and you will see above your search results the rough number of pages that Google has in its index that contains the phrase). We did it (and they are still in the top five), but was this worth the effort and cost?

Generic search terms

Achieving number one positions for broad and generic search terms like this just won't be achievable for most of us (at least in the short term). We won't have the resources (financial or time based) to achieve this. In reality we would also be wasting a lot of time. Who searches for the word 'jobs'? It is most likely to be someone who is assessing the marketplace of recruitment websites. They're at the browsing stage of the online journey and are probably fairly unlikely to be applying for a job on this first visit. In reality, if we start by saying 'I want to be number one for "digital marketing jobs London"', then we start to target people nearer the point of conversion (when they are actually going to do something) and we will be competing against a lot fewer people (588,000 in this particular case, which is a lot better than billions!).

So why would a large organization like the recruitment website I mentioned go for such a generic search term? There are a few reasons outlined below:

- Ignorance – they may not know very much about SEO.

- Long term – it is valid to approach more generic terms in the long term. It is achievable if you're willing to keep working at it and it can make up part of a mixed keyword strategy (this is when you target lots of phrases in lots of combinations on a certain topic).

- Volume – if you sell online advertising you may be more interested in volume than quality. This is because online ads are generally sold CPM (cost per mille or, basically, cost per 1,000 views). The more pages seen, the more money you make, regardless of whether or not the visitor was interested or relevant.

Long tail search

According to SearchEngineWatch, over 50 per cent of searches are done with three or more word phrases. The more specific the phrase we search on, the clearer we are on what we are looking for and the more likely a search is to lead to an action. Some form of action, such as a purchase, download, application, etc is what we generally want to achieve as marketers, so these longer, or *long tail*, phrases are what we should often focus on. The phrase 'long tail' comes from the idea that there is a wide selection of search phrases made up of multiple words that will not drive huge volume (although using multiple long tail phrases can drive lots of traffic), but are more likely to drive conversion (the completion of an online goal such as download, purchase or a form being filled in).

Keyword variations

We also need to understand exactly how people search, and the order and variations of words that they use. Google wants to match exactly what you search for, so the difference between 'Jobs Manchester' and 'Manchester Jobs' is important. Which variation do most people search on? Luckily, Google provides tools that can tell us exactly this – the key two tools are discussed below.

Keyword planner (**https://adwords.google.com/o/KeywordTool**)

The keyword planner (originally known as the keyword tool) is great for finding the actual number (or at least a fairly accurate estimate) of searches for a particular term, which can be looked at globally or country by country. This tool also shows suggested variations of the search term and how many searches these get per month, so it is a fantastic tool for building a list of words that we want to use in order to optimize our pages. Always look at the volume of searches versus how competitive the search term will be. The easiest way to do this is just to search the term and see how many results come back in Google. The higher the number, generally the higher the competition.

FIGURE 6.4   Keyword variations and volumes of searches in the Google keyword planner

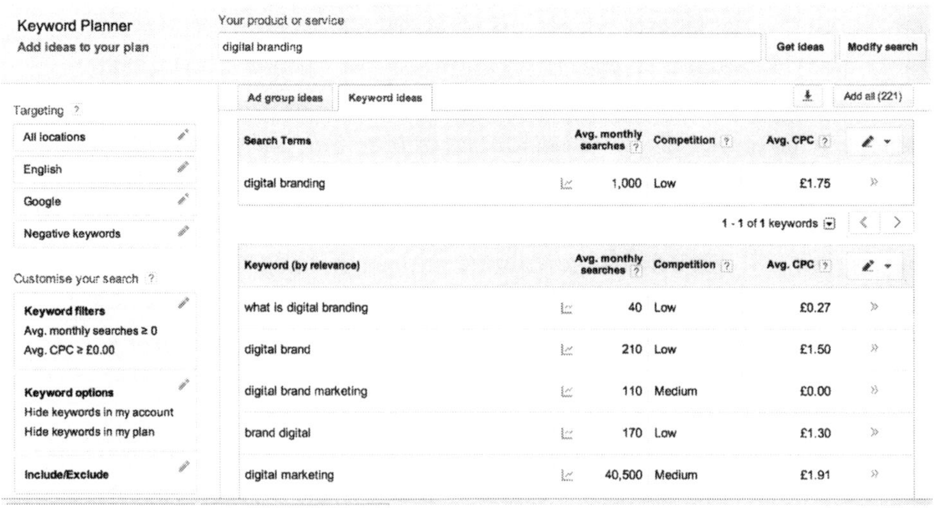

Keyword (by relevance)	Avg. monthly searches	Competition	Avg. CPC
what is digital branding	40	Low	£0.27
digital brand	210	Low	£1.50
digital brand marketing	110	Medium	£0.00
brand digital	170	Low	£1.30
digital marketing	40,500	Medium	£1.91

The screenshot shown in Figure 6.4 shows the results when looking at the phrase 'digital branding'. We are given the number of searches per month and a selection of other related search terms.

Google Trends (**http://www.google.com/trends**)

Google Trends can tell us quite a lot about how people search, but its key capability is in showing trends over time and comparing search terms. Enter a search term and it will show you the trend over time of people searching for that term. It doesn't show an actual number of searches, but rather the trend (the keyword planner tells us actual numbers). We can also enter multiple terms and see how they compare. Its other key capabilities are to show geographical interest in a term by country, which can then be drilled down to by region and city. Always remember that when two countries are compared, it is showing where somebody is more likely to be searching, not necessarily that there is actually a larger volume of searches in that country. Finally, we get a selection of other words that have been searched for in relation to this term, which are the most popular and which have grown most in the past year.

The screenshot in Figure 6.5 shows a comparison of the search terms 'Blackberry', 'Nokia' and 'iPhone' in the UK market. We can see a direct correlation between the market for these brands and the volume of searches for them. Also remember that bad news stories, such as the 'Blackberry Blackout', when the Blackberry network stopped working for a number of days, will also cause a peak in searches.

SEO, local search and Google+

We have already seen the importance of local search, and how maps can dominate the mobile search results for some types of searches. For this reason we need to maximize our opportunities of getting listed on these map-based results. Bing, Yahoo, Baidu, Yandex and Google all allow you to list your location on a map via their mapping services. The more detail you can add to these map-based listings the better, and generally by connecting these listings to your website (which all of these search engines allow you to do) you stand a better chance of showing up in the map results in a mobile search.

FIGURE 6.5 Google Trends comparing search terms

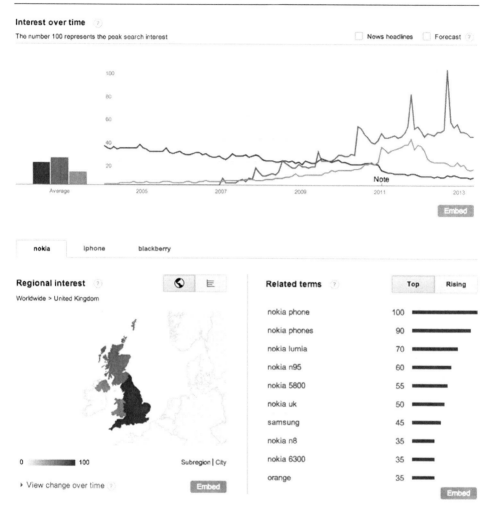

(Google and the Google logo are registered trademarks of Google Inc, used with permission)

Google has taken a different approach, and has merged its local business results into its Google+ platform. Google+ is essentially a social network that offers much of the functionality of sites such as Facebook and LinkedIn. However, at this stage it is worth thinking of Google+ as a social 'layer' on top of search, which gives Google the ability to more precisely match your search requirements to the results that you are given. There are some elements of Google+ that are already changing

FIGURE 6.6   A restaurant listed as a local business result in Google+

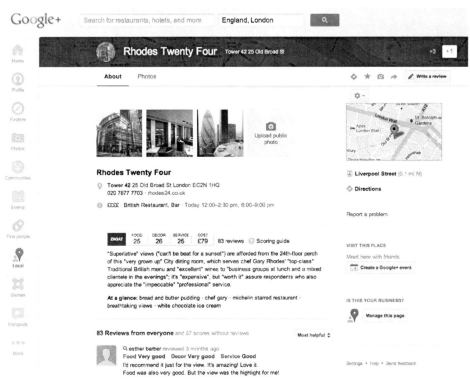

(Google and the Google logo are registered trademarks of Google Inc, used with permission)

search results, and what is clear is that a Google+ local business listing can help you appear in the map results.

The screenshot in Figure 6.6 shows that local business listings, along with map results and reviews, have been automatically turned into Google+ pages. You can also see that on the right-hand side of the screen you can 'Manage this page' by taking ownership, and this allows you to expand and enhance your listings.

On-page optimization

So far we have explored the topics of search engine spiders and keyword research. This means we have made sure that the search spiders can access our web pages and we have identified the words that we want to achieve rankings for. The next stage is to actually get these words onto our pages. On-page optimization is all about getting the right words on the page, in the right place. We have identified the right words during the keyword research phase, and now we need to put them in the right places. This is actually a fairly straightforward process and is just a matter of looking at the core elements of a page and factoring our words and phrases in.

Users first, then search engines

What we are trying to do is help the search engines understand the content on our web pages. However, we don't want to do this at the expense of the user journey. What I mean is that if we over-optimize our content it will actually make our copy hard to read. You can drive all the traffic in the world, but if everyone leaves when they start trying to read your content, you've wasted your time. Focus on getting things right for the user first and then we'll adapt things as appropriate for the search engines.

I've listed below the key areas of the page that are of most importance and then we will look at each of these elements in more detail:

- page title;
- headings;
- web page names;
- copy;
- link text;
- file names;
- alt text.

Each of these different parts of our web pages give us the opportunity to show the search engines what our web pages are all about (see Figure 6.7). So let's take a look at them in a bit more detail.

FIGURE 6.7   The key elements of the page involved in SEO

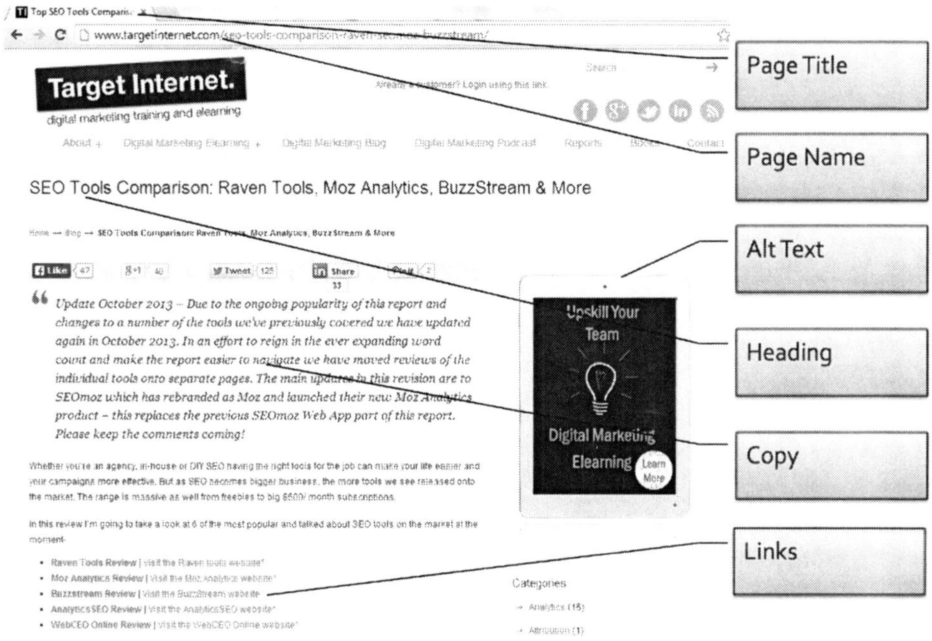

Page title

This is the most important thing on the page, as it is generally given the greatest weighting by the search engines and it is what actually shows up in many search engines (including Google) as the main title in the search engine results pages (SERP) (see Figure 6.8).

FIGURE 6.8   The page title is the main line of the search result in Google

Top **SEO Tools Comparison** & Review - SEOmoz, Raven Tools ...
www.targetinternet.com › Blog ▾
In-depth, impartial review of the best **SEO tools** on the market including SEOmoz, Raven Tools, BuzzStream, AnalyticsSEO, WebCEO, DIYSEO & Advanced Web ...

(Google and the Google logo are registered trademarks of Google Inc, used with permission)

The page title is actually something that shows up in the top bar or tab of your browser window, and is something that most users don't even notice. It is actually something that is initially written by your web developer or content management system (cms), and is one of the most commonly missed and most effective elements of SEO. Huge numbers of website page titles are blank or say things such as 'Home'. In other cases people repeat the same page title again and again, or use their company name. If I'm looking for your company name then that is fine, but what about when I'm searching for what you do? A good page title factors in a range of phrases that a user may search for.

So, for example, 'Online Digital Marketing Training from Target Internet' is a much better page title than 'Target Internet', as it says what my site actually offers and includes the words and phrases that a user might search for.

Headings

The headings and subheadings throughout your pages help the search engines to understand the key themes of these pages. Again, these should factor in the most important words and phrases that a user may be searching for and that you have identified during your keyword research.

The spiders are actually reading the code of your pages. The headings in your copy are represented as H tags. These are part of the HTML code that goes into building your pages, and you actually have up to six different tiers or heading tags. The H1 tag is your main heading, the H2 tag is for subheadings and so on all the way through to H6. In reality, we most often don't get past using H1s and H2s, which is absolutely fine from an SEO perspective. It is important to understand, though, that you should only ever have one H1 but you can have multiple H2s. The logic behind having only one H1 is so that you are clearly indicating the core theme of your page. Multiple H1s would water down this core theme and make it harder for the search engines to understand the real focus of your page. This is a common mistake and should be avoided.

Bear in mind that the actual part of your page that is used as an H1, H2, etc will be decided by either the person who originally coded your page or the CMS that you are using. For this reason it may be necessary to have the code of your pages modified to use the appropriate part of the page as heading tags. Thankfully, in systems such as Wordpress this is all taken care of for you in a very sensible way.

Web page names

Your website address and the actual names of the pages that you create will again act as indicators for the search engines as to what your content is about. This doesn't mean your actual website name must include your keywords, but it does mean that you should name your pages appropriately. For example, my website doesn't have to be called **http://www.digitalbranding.com** if that is the topic of the content (although in an ideal world it would be), but if I create a page on this topic I should name it **www.mywebsite.com/digital-branding**. This is because the search engines are realistic in realizing that many of the addresses for our sites are actually our company names and so on. Again, this may be impacted by your original developer or CMS, and systems such as Wordpress help you to control this easily.

Copy

The main copy on your pages should include your targeted key phrases, ideally in the first paragraph. However, you certainly don't need to keep repeating the words again and again. In fact, if you do repeat the words again and again, not only can you make the copy hard to read, it could actually be interpreted as negative by the search engines (see the information below on 'black hat' SEO).

Black hat versus white hat SEO

What we are talking about is ethical, or so called 'white hat' SEO. This means we are trying to help the search engines to understand our content. There is also something called 'black hat' SEO that is all about trying to manipulate the search engines. If you get caught using black hat techniques you can get completely removed from some search engine results, and Google is particularly effective at detecting these techniques. The main rule is that the website content should be there for the user and not the search engines and that what the user is shown is what the spiders should also see. If you want to understand more about what Google expects and considers to be best practice, take a look at their webmaster guidelines: **http://www.google.com/webmasters**

Link text

The actual words that we link on within our webpages help the search engine to understand the relevance of the page we are linking to (it also to some extent helps set the context of the page we are linking *from*). These actual words we are using to link are referred to as anchor text, and they are an important indicator for the search engines. For this reason we should not use phrases such as 'click here' or 'read more' as these are essentially meaningless to the search engines. These types of phrases also make it harder for a user scanning your page to quickly identify its core themes.

File names

Although only a small factor, the names of the files that make up your pages have some impact on the search engine's understanding of your pages. So you should name your images, video files and so on appropriately to describe their content and, where possible, to factor in your key words and phrases.

Alt text

Alt text is text that describes an image and is put in place by a developer or using a CMS. The alt text is there for accessibility reasons primarily, but also has an impact on SEO. Accessibility is all about making your website usable for people who need to use it in a different way for some reason. For example, if I am a blind user, in order to use the web I will use something called a screen reader, a piece of software that reads out web pages in a simulated voice. When this reader gets to an image, it doesn't understand it, so it reads out the alt text instead. The search engines have a similar problem with images. For this reason they read the alt text in order to better understand the image.

As I have said, the alt text is actually for accessibility, and SEO should be a secondary consideration. However, if you can factor your keywords and phrases into these descriptions, it does help with your overall SEO efforts. You should also be aware that effective use of alt text is very important and is actually a legal requirement within the European Union under the Disability Discrimination Act. Wherever you are based, however, alt tags are important to help people access your website, and they have an impact on SEO.

On-page optimization in perspective

Once you have been through the process of identifying your most important words and phrases, and made sure they have been put within your pages in the appropriate places, you have done the fundamentals of on-page optimization. The search engines get smarter and smarter about understanding how different topics and themes are interconnected, and Google in particular is getting very good at understanding the context, as well as words, of a particular piece of content. For this reason, you should not obsess too much over on-page optimization, but rather focus on providing value through content. That leads us into the extremely important next step in SEO.

Link building

If on-page optimization is telling the search engines what your content is about, link building is telling the search engines the authority of that content. A link to your content from another website is basically seen as a vote of confidence. People only link to content they find useful or interesting, and links are therefore essential to your search optimization efforts.

Neither on-page optimization nor link building can work in isolation, as both are needed in order to understand the topic and authority of your site and its content. Driving more links to increase your authority is all about creating engaging and interesting content, and this is one of the reasons why 'content marketing' has become such an important approach in recent years. If our websites just say how great we are or how great our product is, there is little reason for anyone to link to us. However, if we provide value via our content, we are encouraging links, building value and potentially driving engagement.

For example, my own website's primary commercial aim is to drive enquiries for an e-learning product, but the majority of the site's content is actually about giving free digital marketing advice. This free advice takes the form of blog posts, podcasts and reports. All of this content drives links from other websites where people find this content useful or interesting, and in turn drives my site up the search rankings.

Social signals

As well as looking at the number of links to our content from other websites, the search engines are increasingly concerned with what we call 'social signals'. These social signals are the conversations that are happening in social media about your site and content. This is not to say that you can tweet about your own site a thousand times, however, and that you will suddenly leap to the top of the search rankings! Recall in Chapter 5 that we looked at the social scoring service Klout, which attempts to score the social influence of a particular user or social media account. In reality, the major search engines have an internal process that works in a similar way, and they are trying to access both the quantity and quality of social signals that are being created about your content.

This increasingly means that using social media to get users discussing, engaging with and sharing your content is highly important. Sharing your latest content on the appropriate social platforms can not only create social signals but also encourage further links to your content.

Measuring link authority

There are a number of tools and methods for measuring how effective our link-building strategies are and how authoritative our sites are seen as being. All of these are actually looking at two key things: the quality and quantity of links and social signals to our content.

Search engine algorithms

Much of what SEO agencies concern themselves with is understanding the algorithms that the search engines use to decide how your content is ranked in the search results. In my opinion, this is increasingly a waste of time. The smarter the search engines get, the more complex their algorithms become and the more of a nonsense it becomes trying to decode this set of rules. I was actually told by someone at Google that in reality, even within Google, there would only be a handful of people who know and understand the complete set of rules, because it is such a complicated and huge thing. Rather than focusing on trying to outwit the engineers at Google (good luck with that!), we should focus on the fundamental issue of creating useful and engaging content.

FIGURE 6.9   The excellent Open Site Explorer from Moz.com

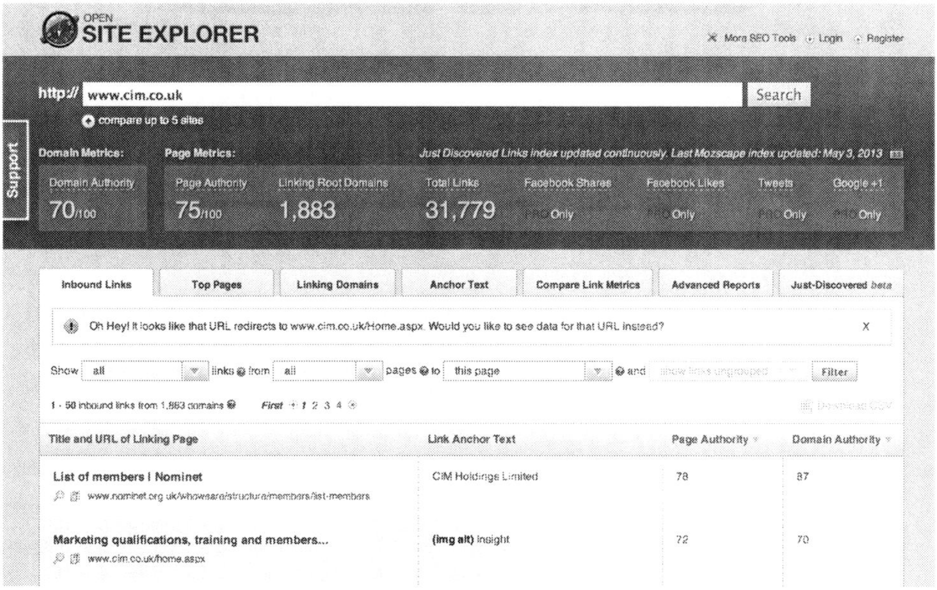

Open Site Explorer

This is an excellent tool from moz.com. moz.com offer a huge range of SEO tools as part of their paid monthly subscription. You can also access Open Site Explorer in a limited way for free. It doesn't give you all of the features, results are limited and you can only use it three times in any one day, but it is still fantastically useful (see Figure 6.9).

When you enter a website or particular webpage into the tool it gives you a range of information about the quantity and quality of links to that page. You are given a score out of 100 for the authority of your domain as well as any particular page you are looking at. It's a great way of benchmarking yourself, and you can do the same for your competitors. The paid version will also show some data on social signals from a limited number of social sites.

Google PageRank

Google's PageRank is a score, given to every web page that Google looks at, between 0 and 10. This score is based on the quantity and quality of links to this content. The quality of the links is in turn based on their PageRank. Therefore, links from websites with a high PageRank help boost your PageRank. PageRank makes up part of the Google algorithm and is an indicator of how much trust or authority Google sees your site and content as having. There is some discussion about how much weighting PageRank is actually given, but we don't need to concern ourselves with that too much at this stage.

There are a number of ways to find the PageRank score for your particular site or page. The first and probably easiest in the long term is to install a plug-in for your browser. I use the Google Chrome browser, and a simple Google search of 'Chrome PageRank plug-in' returns a number of options. Once installed, for every page I visit I can see its score out of 10 in the top right-hand corner of my browser (see Figure 6.10).

Be aware that the PageRank score that we see is always out of date and is only updated a few times per year, but it is still a good long-term indicator. PageRank 7 websites tend to beat PageRank 3 websites in the search rankings every time. It's a fairly blunt measure, but an easy

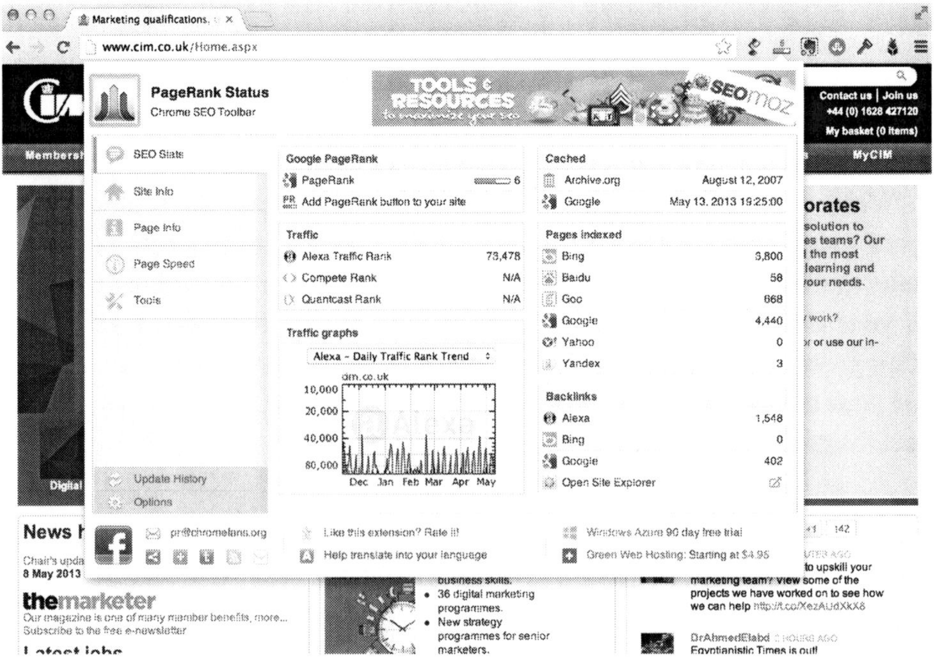

FIGURE 6.10 A PageRank plug-in in action in Google Chrome

one to monitor and should be seen as part of your SEO measurement, not the be all and end all of SEO measurement.

If you're interested in search engines other than Google, such as Yandex or Baidu, they too have their own scoring mechanisms (Yandex, in fact, has its own scoring mechanism called TIC). The reality is that they all look at the quality and quantity of links pointing to your content. Although they all calculate the 'quality' differently, the same core rules apply.

SEO summary

We can sum up mobile SEO into some fairly straightforward key steps:

- User journey – understand what your target audience may be searching for and why. Make sure you understand the user journey and know how search fits in.

- Spiders – make sure that my content is visible to the search engines.

- Keyword research – understand what my target audience is searching for and build a list of words and phrases that I would like to rank for.

- On-page optimization – get these words on my page in the right places.

- Link building – build a content-based strategy to encourage links to and discussions around my content.

- Benchmarking – measure and improve my SEO efforts.

Paid search

Pay per click (PPC) is the other side of search. We'll look at the pros and cons of PPC in detail, but its key advantage is our ability to control and target it precisely.

So how does paid search fit in with branding? It is not about display, that is, it's not the fact that your ad shows up and, even though people don't click on it, it has an impact on your branding by being seen. This is about direct response and driving your audience through to relevant content at an appropriate stage in the user journey. The experience of finding what they are looking for – the experience of what your content offers – is what impacts your digital branding.

If you receive a promise of number one rankings in search from an agency or freelancer, one of two things is happening. They are either talking about PPC, or they are lying. No one can guarantee you number one rankings on Google, even someone who has done it a thousand times before, because only Google control it (see Figure 6.11).

Another major advantage of PPC is speed. You can be number one in the search rankings almost immediately if you are willing to pay for it. Organic search can take months to achieve rankings for competitive terms, and even then it is not guaranteed. Also, don't mistake organic search for being free. Although you don't pay for every click, you will spend time and effort creating content and so on.

PPC is an auction-based system. The more you are willing to pay per click, the more visibility your ad will generally get. This also means that the more competitive your particular industry is, and the words

FIGURE 6.11 Paid search in action in Google

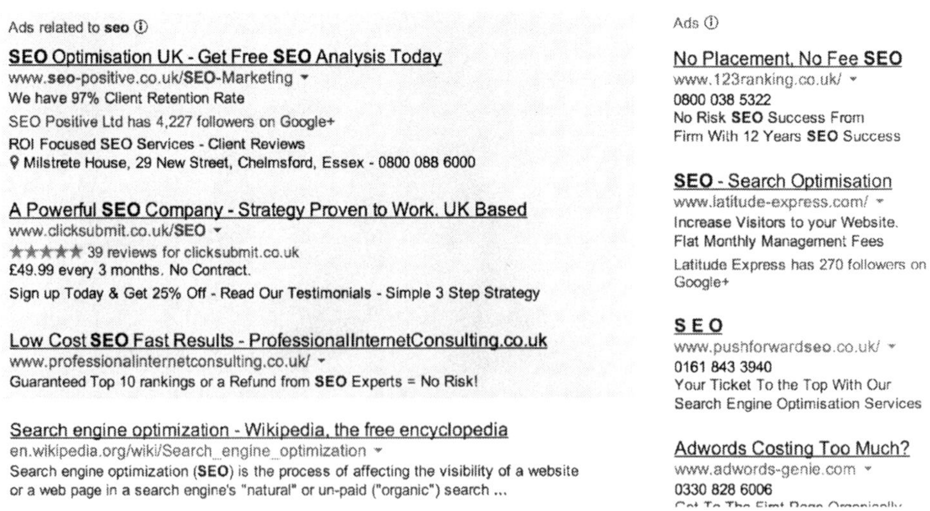

Ads related to **seo** ⓘ

SEO Optimisation UK - Get Free SEO Analysis Today
www.**seo**-positive.co.uk/**SEO**-Marketing ▾
We have 97% Client Retention Rate
SEO Positive Ltd has 4,227 followers on Google+
ROI Focused SEO Services - Client Reviews
♀ Milstrete House, 29 New Street, Chelmsford, Essex - 0800 088 6000

A Powerful SEO Company - Strategy Proven to Work. UK Based
www.clicksubmit.co.uk/**SEO** ▾
★★★★★ 39 reviews for clicksubmit.co.uk
£49.99 every 3 months. No Contract.
Sign up Today & Get 25% Off - Read Our Testimonials - Simple 3 Step Strategy

Low Cost SEO Fast Results - ProfessionalInternetConsulting.co.uk
www.professionalinternetconsulting.co.uk/ ▾
Guaranteed Top 10 rankings or a Refund from SEO Experts = No Risk!

Search engine optimization - Wikipedia, the free encyclopedia
en.wikipedia.org/wiki/Search_engine_optimization ▾
Search engine optimization (**SEO**) is the process of affecting the visibility of a website or a web page in a search engine's "natural" or un-paid ("organic") search ...

Ads ⓘ

No Placement, No Fee SEO
www.123ranking.co.uk/ ▾
0800 038 5322
No Risk **SEO** Success From
Firm With 12 Years **SEO** Success

SEO - Search Optimisation
www.latitude-express.com/ ▾
Increase Visitors to your Website.
Flat Monthly Management Fees
Latitude Express has 270 followers on
Google+

S E O
www.pushforwardseo.co.uk/ ▾
0161 843 3940
Your Ticket To the Top With Our
Search Engine Optimisation Services

Adwords Costing Too Much?
www.adwords-genie.com ▾
0330 828 6006
Get To The First Page Organically

(Google and the Google logo are registered trademarks of Google Inc, used with permission)

that you choose to target, the more expensive it can become. More on this later in this chapter.

PPC fundamentals

The key steps involved in planning and implementing a successful mobile PPC campaign are:

- keyword research;
- create ad copy;
- select additional ad features;
- set targeting criteria;
- set budgets and bids.

PPC keyword research

There will certainly be commonality between this and the keyword research you do for your SEO campaigns, and you will use the same tools. However, one fundamental to understand about PPC is that the more precise your selection of words, and the better matched these are to your ad copy and landing pages, the more successful your campaign will be.

The words you select for your PPC campaigns will trigger your ads. You could select a generic search term to trigger your ad so that you get lots of traffic. This is a very good way to spend lots of money and get little results. You could also use lots of different search terms to trigger the same generic ad. Again a good way to waste your budget. Generally, a very specific key phrase that triggers a specific ad, and which sends the searcher to a very specific and relevant landing page, will get the most from your budget.

Create ad copy

Fundamentally, a PPC ad is made up of a number of lines of text (it may also include an image on platforms such as Facebook) and a link through to your site (or a number of links). This copy is what grabs the searcher's attention and attracts the click through to your site.

We won't go into copywriting techniques here, as much has been written on the topic already, but the wording of my ads need to reflect the right context.

Bear in mind that you can create multiple versions of your ad copy and most PPC systems will automatically rotate these ads and tell you which one is attracting the most clicks and/or conversions on your site.

Paid search and mobile devices

A very important move is Google changing its PPC system (Adwords) to a context-based model. What this means is that we are not just doing one ad for desktop and one for mobile. What we are actually doing is setting up a single campaign that has a number of different options based on the context of your search. That will include what device you are searching on, the time of day and your location. Based on this context I can use different ad options and set my bids accordingly. For a great example of this in action, let's take a look at an example from Google:

Sally's flower shop has a physical shop on Main Street and a website where customers can order online. Within a single campaign, Sally can customize ad headlines, text and landing pages so that people using smartphones see ads that take them to her mobile site, while people using computers and tablets see relevant links on her desktop website.

And when her shop is open, Sally has ads that show links to a shop locator as well as her business phone number for smartphone users. When her shop closes at 5 pm, she sets her ads to only show links to her website, where customers can place their orders. With enhanced campaigns, Sally is able to schedule when and on which devices she would like these ad extensions to appear.

For more on Google Enhanced Campaigns (I'm guessing the name has limited lifetime, as all campaigns are being moved to this format!) take a look at the guide from Google: **http://www.google.co.uk/think/ products/enhanced-campaigns.html**

FIGURE 6.12   Google's Enhanced Campaigns focus on context-based ad campaigns

(Google and the Google logo are registered trademarks of Google Inc, used with permission)

Additional ad features

Google (and Baidu) offers a number of additional ad options to enhance your PPC ads. An example in Google is that you can include links to multiple pages of your website if your ad is in the top positions. Being in these top positions, however, will depend on your bid (how much you are willing to pay for a click). You can also add to your ads links to maps of your location.

These additional ad features serve two purposes. First, they clearly encourage users to take an action in response to your ads. Second, they can make your ad more likely to be noticed in the first place as they differentiate your ad visually and generally add to its overall size.

Set targeting criteria

You can target by the type of device someone is searching on (split between desktop, smartphone and tablet) as well as target by location-based criteria. Location-based targeting is split into three key areas in Google (most other systems follow similar principles, although accuracy can be poor in Baidu in particular):

- targeting by physical location that the search is made in (eg searching for 'hotels' while in New York);

- targeting by what people are searching for (eg searching for 'hotels in New York');

- targeting by intent – this is based on various factors that Google consider, such as previous searches (eg searching for 'hotels' after having searched 'trip to New York' and 'best deals flights New York').

Set budgets and bids

As well as setting your daily budget (the maximum you are willing to spend each day) you can set your maximum cost per click (CPC). CPC is the main factor that decides where your ad shows up on the page. Because PPC systems generally work on an auction basis, the more you are willing to pay per click, the higher up the page your ad appears and the more visibility it has. That visibility should lead to clicks, assuming your ad content is appealing to the searcher. You should not always assume, however, that it is always better to be in the top positions on the page. You may find that being further down the page means you are paying less per click and getting clicks more slowly, but you get better value overall from your budget. This is one of the many reasons that in order to get the maximum value from your budget you need to test and adjust your campaigns on an ongoing basis.

CPC can be set at a number of different levels. You can apply a single maximum CPC to a group of ads or just for a particular key phrase. Many systems, including Google, have an automatic bidding option that will try to maximize the number of clicks you receive for your budget. Just remember, though, that the maximum volume of traffic does not necessarily mean the maximum amount of conversions on your site.

Within Google and their new 'enhanced' campaigns, you can also adjust your bids according to contextual information such as mobile devices and time of day (see Figure 6.13). For example, you may decide that mobile searches are more likely to convert into business, so you may be willing to pay more for a mobile click. You may also find that mobile searches are less competitive than desktop searches and that

FIGURE 6.13   Adjusting bids according to device in Google Adwords

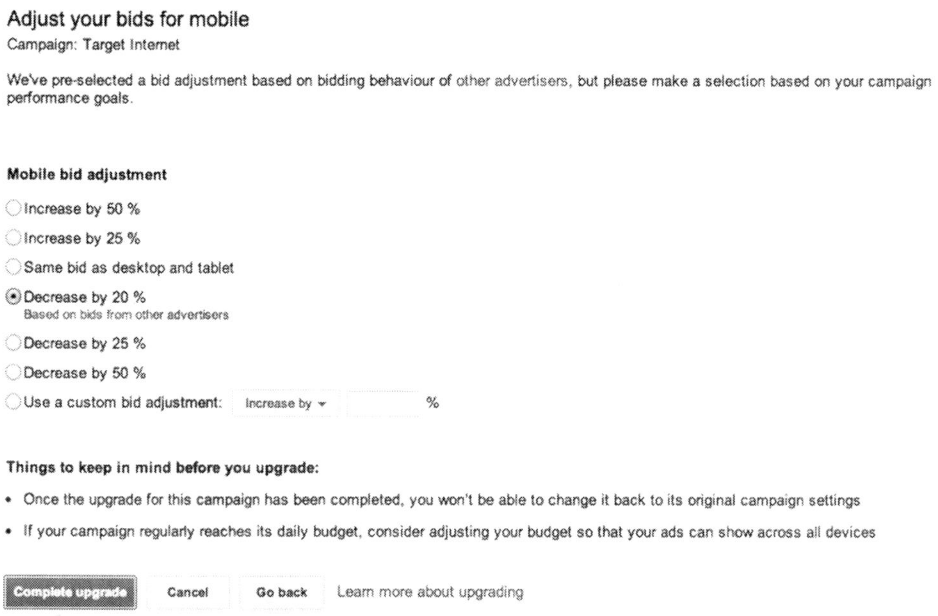

Adjust your bids for mobile
Campaign: Target Internet

We've pre-selected a bid adjustment based on bidding behaviour of other advertisers, but please make a selection based on your campaign performance goals.

Mobile bid adjustment

○ Increase by 50 %

○ Increase by 25 %

○ Same bid as desktop and tablet

◉ Decrease by 20 %
  Based on bids from other advertisers

○ Decrease by 25 %

○ Decrease by 50 %

○ Use a custom bid adjustment: Increase by ▾   %

Things to keep in mind before you upgrade:

- Once the upgrade for this campaign has been completed, you won't be able to change it back to its original campaign settings

- If your campaign regularly reaches its daily budget, consider adjusting your budget so that your ads can show across all devices

[Complete upgrade]   Cancel   Go back   Learn more about upgrading

(Google and the Google logo are registered trademarks of Google Inc, used with permission)

you can actually decrease your bids slightly (my experience is that in most cases currently, you can decrease your bids by 20 per cent and have no impact on your traffic levels, but you need to test this – and it will vary across different key words).

Within Google Adwords you also have the option to set rules-based bidding, meaning that you do things like automatically adjust your bid (within a certain range) to always keep your ad in a certain position. This can help you to automate your bidding in order to factor in changes in competition levels.

PPC considerations

Beyond the fundamentals of PPC, there are some other things we need to consider when planning our campaigns that can have a significant impact on what value we get for our budgets.

Ongoing management and optimization

To get the most out of your PPC budgets your campaigns will need to be closely monitored, tested and adjusted on an ongoing basis. Levels of competition can change, and bids will need to change accordingly. You may find that certain keywords are working well and that others, although driving traffic, are not converting into business. Again, you will need to adjust your campaigns accordingly. This means that as well as considering the cost of your PPC budgets you need to factor in the time or cost of managing your campaigns effectively (we will discuss below using agencies for PPC management).

Quality scoring

The Google Adwords system is particularly focused on rewarding campaigns that are highly targeted and give relevant results to searchers. They do this by factoring in a quality score when deciding what ads to show and how high up the page those ads should be displayed. Quality score takes into account a number of factors but looks at things like the click-through rate (CTR) of your ad in order to signify its relevance. This means that ads that are seen as being relevant are given a boost in their positioning and you can actually have your ad appearing above someone else's who is actually paying more per click than you.

Other quality factors include having the word/phrase that was searched for actually in your ad and on the landing page that you are sending searchers through to. The more relevant your ad, the better your quality score and the more visibility you get for your budget. It also means that Google is rewarding relevant ads, which in turn means that searchers see PPC ads as more relevant generally, and thus should in turn click on the ads more, thus making Google more money. Clever stuff.

Conversion tracking

As with any digital marketing activity, we need to understand what impact it is having on our bottom line. We will discuss the idea of a 'conversion' further in Chapter 14 (The role of analytics), but most PPC systems give you some ability to track beyond a click and see what happens afterwards. After all, all the traffic in the world is useless if the visitors to our site all leave immediately upon arrival.

Working with PPC agencies

Agencies can help you get the most from your PPC budgets by planning and setting up your campaigns effectively and then managing your campaigns on an ongoing basis. They can also add additional cost but bring little benefit. If you plan to work with an agency you need to be very clear on what value they provide and if this is giving you a positive ROI.

From my experience of working with lots of agencies, and having run a search agency, there are a couple of key things to look out for:

- **Payment terms** – far too many PPC agencies charge on percentage of spend basis. So, for example, you pay them 20 per cent of what you are spending on your PPC clicks. This approach makes no sense, for a couple of reasons. First, more money does not necessarily mean more work to manage that budget. It may do, but it is really down to how that budget is being spent. Second, as an agency there is no incentive to save you money and reduce your budget – if that is then going to reduce the agency's fee.

- Another issue to consider is **campaign ownership and handover fees**. What I mean by this is to be very careful of contracts with PPC agencies that state they own the campaign data and/or that there is a handover fee for your campaign. This can mean that you are charged to set up a campaign, but when you cease working with the agency you either have to pay them to hand over the account or start again from scratch. It can also mean that if you part company with the agency that ran your PPC, you no longer have access to the data collected during that campaign, such as which ads/key phrases were performing best, and thus you will need to start the test and learn process from scratch.

- A final consideration: **how much work are you actually getting for your budget?** Many PPC campaigns are managed for a monthly fee, but when the campaign is up and running successfully it is very easy to sit back and just let things tick over without doing any work. For this reason, instead of a monthly bill that just reads 'Campaign Management', you need a breakdown of what work has actually been done. The Google Adwords system can actually track all changes made to a campaign over any given period, which can help you get to the bottom of what work has actually been done. Even when getting these work breakdowns, look out for the catch all 'Keyword Research'. It is a valid activity, but you need to understand what keyword research was actually done and what the output was.

SEO and PPC working together

We need to consider how SEO and PPC can work together effectively as part of our digital branding. I'm often asked whether you should bother with PPC advertising if you are already ranking number one for a search term in the organic search results. The only way to truly get an answer to that question is by testing it. Look at your results with and without PPC running and you answer the question precisely. This testing is even more necessary with mobile search, because of the different user focus and motivations. You will certainly get some cannibalization – that is, people clicking on your paid ads who would have clicked on your organic search results, but you need to understand what additional traffic you can get and then look at how PPC and SEO traffic convert differently.

Search conclusions

Search is an effective and essential part of your digital marketing toolkit and will make up an essential part of the user journey. Therefore, it has a huge impact on our digital branding. Making sure we fully understand our target audience, their motivations and requirements, and mapping this to the content we provide (and optimize), is a fundamental requirement for any organization. This means that effectively planned and implemented search campaigns can be one of our most important business drivers and can have a huge impact on our digital branding.

CASE STUDY   Cadbury – Drumming Gorilla

This campaign was launched in August 2007.

Background

While Cadbury is one of the UK's favourite chocolate brands, it was losing out on sales to Galaxy and so needed to increase brand awareness and reposition itself as the nation's favourite.

The campaign coincided with Cadbury's relaunch of the Wispa bar, which had been decommissioned some years earlier, as well as launching its own brand of gum, Trident, which was hoped would appeal to customers.

Objectives

The brief given to Fallon was to make Cadbury the only brand dedicated to making their customers smile – and that it would form part of a larger campaign known as 'Glass and a Half Full Productions'.

Strategy and execution

The campaign was to last five years and kicked off with the much-loved drumming gorilla ad, which depicted a gorilla playing the drums along to Phil Collins's 'In the Air Tonight' track in front of Cadbury's iconic purple background. The video ends with a picture of a bar of Dairy Milk and the words 'A glass and a half full of joy'.

The ad was developed purely for TV initially, and the execution was carefully planned to ensure it created maximum effect when it launched. A planned teaser campaign saw the ad being promoted in TV listings prior to its airing, which coincided with the Big Brother Final and Rugby World Cup games. When it aired there was already a substantial buzz around it and, for those who hadn't yet seen the ad, it became a subject of excitement and anticipation as to when they would catch it on air.

Fallon were going for fun and they certainly hit the mark, though the ad sparked a lot of debate at the time about its effectiveness. While there was a lot of buzz, it was unclear whether the brand recognition was sufficient. However, the ad has stood the test of time and is still talked about as one of the first attempts to go beyond simply marketing a product to create something entertaining.

The gorilla was followed up with numerous campaigns, including dancing clothes, the 'eyebrows' and the giant chocolate thumbs up, all of which have created a rather endearing quality for the brand and increased support from its customers.

Results

While the ad was posted on Fallon's Vimeo channel, it doesn't actually appear on Cadbury's own YouTube channel, though it has been uploaded by plenty of others. Accordingly, accurate viewing figures are hard to come by.

However, according to Fallon it was the most watched ad on YouTube in 2008 and the most awarded ad globally. The video currently has over 300 'mash-ups' and at least 70 dedicated Facebook groups with over 50,000 fans. For Cadbury, the ad generated a record revenue growth of 7 per cent, which was their best growth for over a decade.

The biggest success for Cadbury was the surge in public support for the brand, which had in previous years suffered a series of media scandals over product contamination and poor advertising choices.

A drumming gorilla who, on the face of it, had nothing to do with chocolate whatsoever and who actually only drummed for one-third of the ad, turned out to be Cadbury's saviour.

Mobile

The main problem with the concept of mobile marketing is that it immediately makes us focus on the device. In reality, this is actually one of the last things we should be thinking about. To put this in context we can try to answer a couple of questions. How big does my phone have to be before it is a tablet? How about if the screen on my laptop flips over and is a touch screen, is it then a tablet?

The reality is that the lines between mobile and non-mobile devices is blurring and will continue to do so as technology changes (we already have a device that is somewhere between a mobile and a tablet that is being referred to as a 'phablet' (this is by far one of my least favourite new words to come out of the mobile world!). What this tells us is that mobile marketing is not all about the device, it is about the changing user journey. As I've said repeatedly, we need to focus on and understand the user journey in order to maximize our digital branding efforts. What it means is that our digital branding needs to take into account the changes to the user journey caused by mobile devices.

This alignment with the user journey and what the consumer actually wants is essential, and although it sounds obvious, is more often than not completely missed in mobile marketing campaigns. The reason that this basic concept of alignment with consumer requirements is missed is that we (or the partners and agencies we work with) are blinded by the technology and creative options.

Technology for the sake of technology

Just because we can build an app doesn't mean we should (in fact you really need to think about mobile sites before apps in the majority of cases, but more on that later). Using technology inappropriately without setting objectives or having a clear business case is nothing new.

From my experience, the majority of business Twitter and Facebook accounts are set up with little or no idea as to why it is being done. It happens because someone senior has decided it is a good idea without understanding it, someone junior did it without asking anyone, or someone in the business has seen that competitors are doing it and so feels that an opportunity is being missed. It doesn't mean that it is necessarily the wrong channel or a bad idea, but anything done without objectives or a business case is generally doomed to failure.

User journey and context

I've mentioned the user journey a few times already, but let's try to understand this in a bit more detail. We need to understand what our target audience might want to achieve, understand their path to doing this, see how mobile fits in and then provide the right experiences and content to achieve these objectives.

Some of this will be the *discovery phase* (also referred to as 'push', 'stimulus' and in a dozen other ways!) where we are trying to build awareness, educate and stimulate some form of further action. Some will be in the *engagement phase*. These are activities that are driving engagement, experiences and moving towards the user's final objectives (see Table 7.1).

TABLE 7.1 Discovery and engagement phases in mobile marketing

Discovery phase	Engagement phase
Mobile e-mail	Mobile sites
Mobile display ads	Apps
Mobile paid search	Mobile optimized social media
Mobile organic search	Mobile payment and couponing
Offline stimulus (QR codes, etc)	Location-based interaction (NFC, etc)
Push notifications	

The line between discovery and engagement becomes increasingly blurred as we move into location-based interaction (engaging with a brand when in-store, for example), but these phases can start to lay a foundation for us when thinking about where mobile fits into the user journey. However, this is currently a fairly one-dimensional model that only really talks about mobile marketing techniques, while acknowledging that things like offline marketing may exist.

Local intent

I have so far left out mentioning the local-based consumer. Not because this type of consumer is not important, but because it can be a distraction from the broader picture. If your business has any sort of location-based offering it can be immensely powerful, but this goes back to our concept of understanding the target audience's objectives and context, and then using mobile technologies to deliver the most appropriate solution.

According to Google, 94 per cent of smartphone users have carried out a local search (Google Mobile Playbook, 2012). If I am looking for a local hotel, my nearest bus stop, a nearby provider of power supplies for my brand of laptop and so on, this type of search is transformational to the mobile user and any potential business involved.

Integrated devices

Our expectations of mobile device are radically different now and smartphones and tablets offer us fully integrated computing and telecommunications devices. This integration is what has led to the radical change in usage that we need to understand in order to make best use of mobile marketing.

When we consider the level of internet searches done on mobile devices, social media interactions and e-mail reading and writing (all of which we will explore in a moment), we quickly see that what we are doing with the device becomes far more important.

The technology distraction

It is easy to get bogged down in working out which mobile devices your app should work on, what happens when a new phone version comes out and how effective your responsive design website is. All of this stuff matters because of the final outcome of your mobile campaigns, but the reality is that your mobile consumers don't care. They just want to be able to get stuff done.

Responsive design means absolutely nothing to the majority of the people on this planet and nor should it (and maybe to you right now, so we'll talk about this more in a moment). You need to worry about the technical aspects of your mobile strategy but your users shouldn't. They shouldn't even notice it.

Mobile compatible is not mobile optimized

Just because your website works on mobile devices does not mean it is mobile optimized. What I mean is that the site may load up fine on my phone, but if I have to zoom in a dozen times to see anything clearly, this isn't an optimal experience.

What we need to consider now is what my target audience is likely to do, in what context and on what devices. I can then start to make sure I have ticked the appropriate boxes to make their experience as pain free as possible.

With regard to the amount of time it takes for a site to load, users are even more impatient on mobile devices than they are when using a desktop or laptop (KissMetrics, 2013). They have come across so many poor mobile sites that they just give up very quickly. On the other hand, if we can create a seamless mobile experience we stand a better chance of achieving our objectives and can actually build loyalty.

Technology challenges

So, you're thinking something along the lines of: 'It's all very good saying the technology doesn't matter, but I have to make choices and every time I make a change it costs money.' You're 100 per cent right. The reality is that this has always been the case in marketing. We have to decide where to spend our money and how to prioritize our budgets. The actual problem here is that the number of options is large and we don't ask the right questions.

Asking the right questions

Rather than asking should you build an Android, iOS or a Blackberry app (if you have no idea what I'm talking about, take a look at the box below), we should actually be asking what devices your target audience use and which groups it will be most cost-effective to reach. Let's frame this for a moment by forgetting about mobile. If I decide I am targeting an audience but I can only afford to target 50 per cent of it, I need to decide which 50 per cent. I don't do this based on an opinion, I most likely do it on the potential lifetime value of that customer, how much it will cost to target them and other commercially-focused criteria. The same applies to the different mobile platforms and choices we make within our mobile strategies.

Platform wars

It's worth understanding the key players in the mobile operating system (OS) market. For the sake of simplicity we've just looked at the major smartphone and tablet platforms here. An OS is just the software that a phone runs on and will impact its functionality and, most importantly for us, apps built for one platform generally don't work on another. The key players are:

- *Android*: Google's mobile OS. It is open source, meaning it can theoretically be used and adapted by anyone. It has also been adopted by the Open Handset Alliance (OHA), which includes big handset manufacturers such as Samsung, Sony and HTC.

- *iOS*: Apple's OS used on its iPhone, iPod, AppleTV and iPad product range. It is closely associated with OS X used on Apple Mac computers.

- *Blackberry*: Blackberry's OS for all Blackberry devices.

- *Windows Phone*: Microsoft's OS is used by several handset manufacturers, including Nokia on their Lumia range of phones. It is not compatible with Windows for PCs.

Beyond these platforms with the largest market share there are a whole lot more. Take a look at Wikipedia to see just how many (and then don't worry about them! By the way, if you are going to send me hate mail about telling people to ignore your particular mobile OS of choice, you should probably get out more): **http://wikipedia.org/wiki/Mobile_operating_system**

Audience segmentation

Just because 40 per cent of the world use a particular type of mobile OS, it doesn't mean that your target audience in your target market do. For this reason you shouldn't rely on a lot of the generalized statistics that are published. If you do need some initial guidance, take a look at the next chapter, which tries to summarize the key trends and statistics from each region of the world.

In reality, your target audience probably won't align with the norms of your particular market, and if you are working across multiple regions it clearly gets more complicated. What we really need to do is to collect some actual market insights, as we should with any other aspect of our marketing. You can do this by sample surveying your target audience and actually asking the question as to which type of mobile OS they use.

Frictionless technology

What we are aiming for is to make the process of achieving the consumer's goal as simple and as transparent as possible. This idea of making the process as seamless as possible is often referred to as 'frictionless technology'. What we should always consider in our mobile marketing is what the objective of the user is, and how that can most effectively be achieved using the right technology in the right place.

Mobile sites and responsive design

Let's make something clear from the outset: you need a mobile optimized site. That doesn't mean that your site happens to work on mobile devices: it means the user journey via mobile has been carefully considered and you offer the optimal experience via mobile devices. It means that you have weighed up the different technical solutions in order to achieve this and have selected the most appropriate approach. It also means that you have not been steered by the limitations of your current web platform or content management system (CMS).

Start with the fundamentals

Already, an average of 23 per cent of visitors to many sites are visiting on mobile devices (Walker Sands, 2013). This means that, potentially, nearly one-quarter of your audience will be on a mobile device. This is reason enough to make sure that your site is fully optimized for these visitors, before you even consider the potential of increased conversion rates and average order values via a properly optimized mobile experience. Increased average order values of up to 22 per cent have been demonstrated through properly optimized mobile experience (Affiliate Window, 2013).

Focus on the user journey

The key point of a mobile optimized site is to offer an experience that best suits the consumer's needs and setting. This means they should be able to access the information or utility that your site offers, on the device they are using, in an easy and efficient way.

Responsive design

Responsive design, sometimes referred to as adaptive design (although these definitions actually mean different things, as explained below), means developing one site that will display differently on different devices. This means that the site can look completely different on

FIGURE 7.1   A great example of responsive design in practice showing the CSS-Tricks website. On the left the full width version, on the right the same site with the browser width reduced. http://www.css-tricks.com

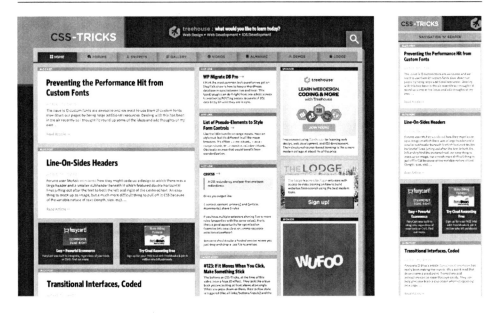

different devices and will layout in a way best suited to a particular device.

This approach is generally implemented using a combination of web technologies. The key point is that these technologies allow the browser to look at things such as the device that the site visitor is using, the width and height of the display, and then decide on how the page should be laid out (see Figure 7.1).

Responsive versus adaptive

Responsive design and adaptive design are often terms that are used interchangeably, yet they are quite distinct.

Responsive design is something that is actioned within your browser. This means that a page is sent to your browser and your browser then does the work to display the correct elements of the page. This is called a 'client side' technology (the client is your browser).

Adaptive design is something that is actioned on the web server. The type of device being used is discovered and then the appropriate version of the site is delivered. This is called a 'server side' technology.

The advantage of adaptive design is that not as much content is sent to your browser, where it may not be used, and a solely mobile version of a site is sent to a mobile device. See the box below, 'Points of view', on responsive design and its limitations).

The term 'responsive design' is gradually coming to mean adaptive design, although developers will argue about the differences for ever more.

Mobile apps

At the time of writing, the Apple app store has just passed 50 billion downloads and Apple is paying more than US $1 billion per month to app developers (Forbes, 2013). This app 'gold rush', as it has been described, has led to a flurry of activity in the world of app development and the production of millions of apps.

Many organizations rushed out and built apps just because they could. I witnessed dozens of conversations that started with the words 'We need an app' and ended in protracted discussion about what it could do, and how much it would cost. Just as we discussed in Chapter 5 on social media, however, just because you can do something doesn't mean that you should.

Mobile sites first

If you don't have a mobile optimized website, forget about getting an app built and get the mobile optimized website fixed first. We have already talked about the huge increase in traffic to sites on mobile devices, and the reality is that this is actually more likely than an app to be a user's initial experience of your mobile presence. It's not that apps aren't also important, and in fact some studies have found that 85 per cent of users prefer the experience of apps over mobile sites (Compuware, 2013), but in reality if you actually need an app, you most likely also need a mobile optimized site.

Bolstering value proposition

Just like any marketing activity we need to start by aligning our business objectives with user requirements and decide how our app can help achieve this. One thing that apps can be fantastic at is bolstering value proposition by delivering some form of online utility or entertainment.

Mobile conclusions

Mobile is not about the device, it's about a changing user journey. For our digital branding to be effective we need to embrace these changes and the potential added complexity that this presents. It means that the technology behind our websites needs to adapt quickly to the changing devices that our audience will be using, but this needs to be seamless to their experience.

Points of view – Jess Butcher, co-founder and CMO, Blippar

Jess is an extremely well respected entrepreneur and co-founder of the extremely popular augmented reality platform Blippar. She very generously shared her thoughts with us around the impact of platforms like Blippar on digital branding and how we can approach measurement (I should also point out that she did this in the week running up to her maternity leave, so I am extremely grateful!).

If you're not familiar, Blippar allows you to 'blipp' real-world objects and for this to launch some form of experience on your mobile device. The object does not need a QR code or anything similar. It's definitely worth a download to see some great inspirational campaign ideas. See **http://www.blippar.com**

How does Blippar contribute to the user journey and how does this impact brands and measures like brand awareness and front of mind awareness?
Where no direct conversion mechanic exists (ie instant purchase, or m-coupon), then the medium is used to brand build – and provides an excellent, immersive, memorable experience with a brand for the user.

Few other advertising medium-types win the consumer's proactively-requested, undivided attention in such an interactive manner (eg game play, quizzes, polling, etc), nor for a dwell-time of up to five minutes in some cases.

Where do you think Blippar is in regard to adoption and how have you approached trying to get increasing use of the technology?
Currently at 3 million downloads globally – but achieved through only around 500–600 campaigns. Acquisition is via partner and media campaigns and soon to launch self-publishing tools for brands/agencies and media-owners will see each partner able to publish this volume of content themselves. So we're expecting to see downloads increase exponentially.

How do you see brands progressing with digital?
Technically, our medium is not digital anyway. It's a way of digitizing the physical, traditional media – so breathing new life into it and bridging the gap between digital and offline.

How can you demonstrate ROI with a technology platform like Blippar?
We can look at measures like total interactions, unique interactions, dwell-time and then look at how these impact purchase intent.
We can also approach this from an ROI on media spend. This means we can equate interactions to different creative media-buying options, eg outdoor versus press versus online. However, we can also geolocate usage, which adds another level of understanding. Where possible we can also look at direct actions such as purchase, coupon download/ redemption, data sign-up, eg for sweepstake/competition, geolocation request for nearest store etc.

Online advertising

Let's start by being cynical (or perhaps realistically pragmatic!). Online advertising is probably the easiest aspect of digital marketing to waste your budget on and carry out ineffective campaigns. This is because banner ads are the easiest part of our digital branding to understand from a traditional advertising perspective. This means that many traditional marketers' approach to digital has been to create print/TV ads and then create digital equivalents of these in a banner format. This approach is generally poorly targeted and not adjusted accordingly for the digital channel it is delivered through. Much of the blame for this lies with agencies that don't really understand digital, but also because it is a channel that lends itself to a 'broadcast' approach. I have said that justifying marketing activity of which we could calculate the return is often put down to 'brand building' and this has been particularly true of banner ads. As click-through rates go down, we persuade ourselves that it is not about the click, but we do little to measure its effectiveness. We will remedy that in Part Three, but in this chapter we look briefly at the key factors involved in online advertising and how they impact our digital branding.

The positive side of online advertising is that we now have a wide range of creative and targeting options that can improve the effectiveness of our ads, along with the analytics and metrics to judge their success. I am not against online advertising, but it is always wise to keep your eye on the end objective.

Online advertising is fundamentally about various forms of banner advertising, including video ads and, as mentioned in Chapter 6, paid search is a form of advertising. In fact, due to the amount of different creative options, the term 'banner advertising' doesn't really cover all of the different things we can do with digital ads.

Advertising objectives

Just like any other aspect of digital branding we should start by clearly defining what our actual end objectives are and how online advertising is going to contribute to these goals. The reason this is even more important to define when considering online ads is because of the way they are often priced and measured.

Most online advertising is sold on a cost per mille (CPM) basis. This basically means that you pay a certain fee every time your ad is shown 1,000 times. This means that you are paying for display, not even clicks, and certainly not for results. This isn't the only option, but it is the most common. The result is that it is very easy to waste budget on views of your ad that are seen by the completely wrong audience.

Your ad being shown once is called an 'impression'. If I hit refresh 10 times on a page with an ad on it, that will be 10 ad impressions. Also, if a page loads that my ad is on, but the ad is below the fold (below the part of the page that I can see without scrolling down), and the user doesn't scroll down the page, the ad will still have had an impression even though no one saw it. The impression also doesn't tell you how long the user was actually on the page that the ad was shown on. This page view duration is referred to as 'dwell-time', and even if my dwell-time was half a second, if the ad loaded, an impression gets counted. We clearly need to look carefully at what we are paying for.

Another challenge with online advertising is that results are often measured on a click-through rate (CTR) basis. The reality, though, is that even if we get clicks it doesn't mean that the visitor who drives to your site will necessarily carry out the action that you want them to. They may leave your site as soon as they arrive. Equally, someone who doesn't click on your ads may interact with them in some way and go on to make a purchase. This means that we need to find better ways than CTR to measure the success of an ad.

App advertising

As well as the options for advertising on mobile sites, we also need to consider ads within apps. This may be from the perspective of running ad campaigns in appropriate apps that are used by your target audience, but it may be from the perspective of making money by placing ads within your apps.

Both Apple and Google have mobile ad platforms to allow you to sell advertising space in your apps (iAds and AdMob respectively) and on both iOS and Android you can integrate ads from a wide variety of different ad networks (more on this later). All of these solutions generally work by automatically placing ads within your apps (in the locations you have developed into the app) and then giving you a share of the revenue made from the ads.

If you want to advertise within apps, then there are a number of different ad networks you could go to (again, more on this later) or you could approach an app owner directly to negotiate a deal.

Ad networks versus media owners

An ad network manages the advertising space on a number of different mobile properties that may include both mobile sites and apps. These ad networks may also manage advertising space on desktop sites. They offer a range of targeting options and then place your ads within the sites they manage according to your targeting criteria. Different ad networks have different targeting criteria, which can vary from fairly basic options such as category matching (automotive, finance, etc) all the way through to things such as behavioural targeting.

Generally, ad networks charge a fee and then share some of this with the owner of the location that the ads are shown in. They provide the technology for placing the ads, the account management to the advertisers and provide some form of reporting for all parties involved.

Ad networks are why there are standard sizes and types of ads. This means you can create an ad once and it can be run across multiple properties (mobile sites and apps) without the need to redesign every time.

Internet Advertising Bureau

The Internet Advertising Bureau (IAB) is the trade association for online and mobile advertising. It promotes growth and best practice for advertisers, agencies and media owners. They have sites for regions around the world sharing best practice and define the standards for sizes and types of ads. This includes the various types of mobile ads, and defines things such as how big they should be in regard to screen size, file size, etc.

The global website can be found at **http://www.iab.net**, and they also have local market sites, which are listed on the main website.

Rather than going to an ad network, you could go directly to a media owner. A media owner in mobile marketing is someone who owns a site or app (or even e-mail list) that you may wish to advertise on. Going directly to a media owner has the advantage of knowing exactly where and how your ads will be shown (this often isn't true when using ad networks, because much ad placement is 'blind placement', meaning you set the targeting criteria but don't get to choose the exact sites that your ads show on). The disadvantage is that very often you are targeting one site or app at a time and they don't have the targeting technologies available via the ad networks. They may also be limited in the types of creative options they offer and the reporting facilities they provide.

Targeting options

Different ad networks offer different types of ad targeting, and I've summarized the most common of these below. One network normally doesn't offer all of the options, and different networks will have access to place advertising on different websites. Thus you may need to work with multiple ad networks to achieve your campaign objectives. The most common types of targeting are:

- **Location:** place your ads based on location-based criteria such as country, city and distance from a physical location. This option can often also be used to exclude as well as include an area.

- **Demographic:** target by criteria such as age and gender. This may be based on users having registered their details or it may be based on some sort of modelling basis, in which case it is worth understanding how this data is modelled and how likely the data is to be accurate.

- **Category:** one of the simplest forms of targeting, based on the category of the content within the site or app. For example, automotive, finance, etc.

- **Content matched:** the content of the page the ad is being placed on is read and ads are matched based on content. This is how ads are placed within Google's display network (discussed in Chapter 6). This can be effective, but just because I am reading a news story about pirates doesn't mean I want to buy a boat!

- **Behavioural:** there are lots of different approaches to behavioural targeting, but generally these rely on being able to see a user's behaviour across a website (or number of websites) and then targeting ads accordingly. I may be looking at an automotive website, but if I have just been on three websites looking at credit card deals, then it is perfectly valid to show me an ad for a credit card on the automotive website.

- **Re-targeting:** this allows you to show ads to users who have visited your site before. So, for example, if I visit your site but don't buy anything, I could then be shown ads for your site on other websites.

Creative options

This is where things start to get very interesting. The amount of different creative options for mobile ads is exploding. A few of the more common options are listed below, along with a pointer to where to find some great resources for getting creative inspiration (a black and white book doesn't really do interactive online advertising full justice!):

- **Banners:** images can be displayed with or without animation, and users can tap the banner to be taken to a variety of destinations.

- **Expandable:** expands an ad to cover the full screen upon a tap, without removing the user from the app or mobile browser experience.

- **Interstitial:** displays full-screen rich media ads either at app or mobile browser launch or in between content pages.

- **Video:** various options to place video before/after/during other video content or within other rich media formats.

- **Mobile:** the IAB's 'Rising Stars Ad Units' (see Figure 8.1) highlights some of the new and highly interactive mobile ad formats, and generally gives videos to show how they work in action. These ad formats have great creative opportunities but are not necessarily widely available.

FIGURE 8.1   The IAB's 'Rising Stars Ad Units'

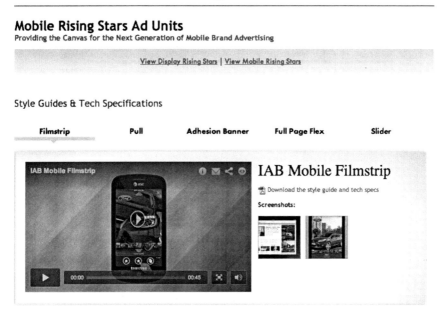

Ad reporting and analytics

Most ad networks will provide reporting tools, but ideally we should integrate our advertising data with our mobile and app analytics so that we can get an integrated view of our mobile marketing efforts.

An initial step is to make sure that all of our mobile ads are tagged with analytics tracking code. This allows us to identify any traffic coming from our mobile ads to our sites and apps and then track this through to conversion. Instructions on how to do this for Google Analytics is outlined in Chapter 14.

Taking things a stage further, Google now allows you to import data from other ad networks and platforms into Google Analytics so that you can compare and contrast data in one place. This functionality can be found under the traffic sources reports and is currently titled Cost Analysis.

Google analytics and single customer view

Google realizes the importance of having all of our sources of data from digital marketing in one place so that we can effectively manipulate and analyse the data to make smarter marketing decisions. Cost Analysis and various announcements made recently indicate their plans to keep Google Analytics as the place to get your single customer view, allowing users to bring in and connect more third-party data sources into the Google environment.

Online advertising conclusions

The mobile advertising market is currently highly fragmented with a high range of ad targeting, features and creative options. Just like any form of banner advertising, the results of campaigns are highly variable based on the options used and the overall effectiveness of approach. For this reason, any online advertising efforts should be carefully considered and tied back to business objectives, with a clear methodology put in place from the outset for tracking and measuring results.

The varied, and often highly interactive, creative options available are very impressive. However, if we go back to our initial concerns about user objectives, we need to ask some very searching questions before making assumptions about the effectiveness of any online advertising campaigns.

It is very easy to be sold online advertising on the basis of its 'brand impact'. Don't forget it is one of many touchpoints and, as the easiest to understand from a traditional advertising and branding point of view, it is often over-relied on. Map out the user journey, work out where it fits in and then measure for success.

E-mail marketing

More often than not, e-mail marketing is not seen as part of your branding efforts, other than in terms of the design used for how the e-mail is presented. I couldn't disagree more. E-mail is one of the most personal and adaptable forms of digital marketing and, when done well, gives us a huge opportunity to engage and influence. Unfortunately, it is also very easy to do badly.

If we go back to the idea that your brand is the sum of all of the experiences or touchpoints that you have with an organization, product, etc, then e-mail can be a highly targeted and direct touchpoint. The problem is that most e-mail is poorly targeted, badly designed and not at all personalized. In this chapter we explore how we can make the most of e-mail marketing as part of our digital toolkit. In Chapter 10 we will explore how we can take this even further with customer relationship management (CRM) integration and marketing automation systems.

E-mail isn't exciting

I don't agree with this statement one bit, and I'll explain why in a moment, but let's start with an example. If I run a webinar or a conference talk and I include the phrase 'social media' I am fairly sure I'll fill the room (virtual or otherwise). However, if we talk about some element of e-mail marketing, it just won't get the same level of response. Most of us are interested in what's new and what's changing, and many of the core principles of e-mail marketing have been the same for some time. The issue is that not many of us are following these principles and we would rather try something new than improve what we are already doing.

Ease of iteration

The single greatest thing about e-mail, in my opinion, is the ability to test, learn and change quickly and easily. Trying different versions of pages on your website or creating different apps can be expensive, time consuming and often fraught with technical problems. Trying different e-mail subject lines, calls to action and length of copy are all extremely easy to test, assuming you are using the right e-mail service provider (ESP).

An ESP will allow you to store e-mail lists, create and send e-mail campaigns and track results: how well-suited your ESP is to your needs will have a direct impact on how effective your e-mail campaigns can be. There are dozens of different ESPs out there, ranging from basic through to highly sophisticated systems that could be used as CRM systems in their own right. We'll explore what we need from an ESP in more detail in a moment, but first we need to look at the state of the e-mail market and dispel some myths.

The state of e-mail marketing

It would be very easy to jump to the conclusion that e-mail marketing is on the decline – for two key reasons. First, social media allows for all kinds of interactions that previously we may have used e-mail for. For example, I certainly don't e-mail my friends any more. Also, we're always hearing complaints about e-mail spam – what a huge problem it is and how all e-mail accounts receive a deluge of it. This may be true to some extent, but before we jump to any conclusions we really need to look at the actual numbers and understand how people are using e-mail.

The Direct Marketing Association (DMA) carried out their annual e-mail tracking report and found that the number of people receiving e-mails from brands they trust remains at a stable 90 per cent and that consumer approval of e-mail marketing has remained the same for the last 12 months, with 28 per cent saying that more than half the e-mails they receive are relevant to them (DMA E-mail Tracking Report, 2013).

Interestingly, the same study looked at mobile usage and found that for 75 per cent of consumers, desktop/laptop was the primary access device for e-mail. However, 57 per cent said they also access their e-mail on a smartphone device. The most telling figure was that 68 per cent said they would wait until they were on their desktop/laptop to make an online purchase. This is a clear indication that the mobile experience isn't matching up to consumers' requirements in terms of trust or convenience. There is also a clear difference between general consumer usage and business use of e-mail, with 47 per cent of all e-mails being opened on a mobile device, according to Litmus (E-mail Analytics, Litmus, 2013).

So why are we seeing such large differences between reported statistics on e-mail marketing and how many of us are using a mobile device to read our e-mails? It really comes down to one of the key principles we need to embrace with e-mail, and that is that every e-mail list is different and will respond slightly differently. Although at first this sounds problematic, in that we can't make too many assumptions about the behaviour of people on our lists, it is in fact one of the greatest things about e-mail. I can learn what works for my target audience and adjust things over time. What kind of subject lines do my audience respond to? How likely are they to share content via social media once I have e-mailed them? What is the correct length of e-mail to send? The list of variables goes on and on, and this is something we'll explore more when we look at testing later in this chapter.

We know that consumers are still using e-mail, but what about the marketing industry? Are we still embracing e-mail marketing? According to DMA both B2B and B2C brand marketers are confident that e-mail expenditure will rise over the coming 12 months (DMA National Client E-mail Report, 2013/14).

So consumers are using e-mail, the industry is confident, but what about the issues with spam that we talked about earlier? Actually, the amount of spam we are receiving is going down (although I know it often doesn't feel like it). Although spam still accounts for more than 70 per cent of all e-mails it is down from over 85 per cent in 2012 (SecureList, 2013). Bear in mind that this is detected spam, which means it will have been filtered from your inbox one way or another. This decline in spam is down to two key factors: 1) advances in technology in detecting and filtering spam so that it doesn't reach us in the first place; and 2) we are generally wising up to spam, which makes it less effective.

Another thing worth understanding is how spammers achieve much of their e-mail volume and why security organizations can have such a big impact on their capability. Spammers don't sit there sending huge volumes of e-mails from their own systems, as this would be easily detected and they would be shut down very quickly. What they actually do is use various forms of malware (malicious software) to allow them to hijack other people's computers and send e-mails from them. These systems of hijacked computers are known as botnets.

The decline of spam and rise of BACN

You are probably very aware of the concept of spam, defined as unsolicited e-mail communications. As we have said, spam is actually on the decrease and a range of security and technology solutions are helping to progress this fight. What is generally on the rise, though, is BACN (pronounced bacon). BACN is defined as the range of e-mails that we have signed up for but don't see as relevant and never read. Over time we subscribe to more and more newsletters, we get service and social media updates that we never read, and are generally getting more e-mail, which although not truly spam is not relevant or useful to us.

Increasingly, web-mail clients such as Gmail are trying to separate this kind of e-mail from e-mails that are relevant, by placing these e-mails under separate tabs. Different systems have different ways of judging the relevance of an e-mail, but very often it is based on user behaviour. If you regularly open and click on e-mail from a particular address, these systems will learn your behaviour and identify that an e-mail is relevant and they are more likely to place this e-mail in your main inbox. Therefore, getting engagement and clicks on every one of your e-mails becomes even more important as it will impact on whether your future e-mails are seen.

FIGURE 9.1   Gmail's tabbed e-mail in action, separating key e-mails from social messages and promotional messages

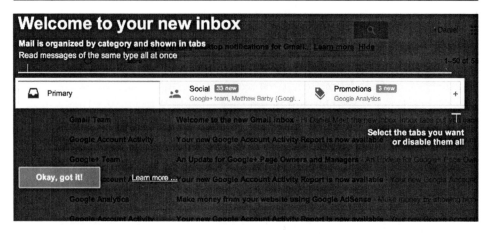

(Google and the Google logo are registered trademarks of Google Inc, used with permission)

It is not just the security companies that are fighting back against e-mail spammers, however. Many e-mail systems, including Google's widely used Gmail, not only filter spam but also try to separate your most important e-mail from other types of e-mail, such as social messages and newsletters. This is achieved using tabbing and some smart filtering (shown in Figure 9.1). The aim is not only to get rid of the spam, but also to separate the essential e-mails from your less important content and the BACN.

Focusing on relevance

This movement towards separating essential e-mails from promotional e-mails means that if we use e-mail as a broadcast channel, focusing on sales messages, we are likely to get lower and lower response rates. We need to focus on using a range of techniques and technologies available to us to make our e-mail as tailored, relevant and useful as possible to our audience, and that's what we'll explore in this chapter.

This doesn't mean that you can't send promotional e-mails with products and special offers. If I ask you to send me special offers, then that is what you should do, but they need to be the right offers for me, sent at the right time and at the right level of frequency. And if I've signed up for a newsletter, don't just send me sales messages. The general approach I apply to e-mail marketing when not working on an e-commerce basis, and an immediate online sale is not the proposed outcome, is to consider the principles of content marketing. There should be a ratio of commercial and non-commercial content in your e-mails, and by that I mean really providing value through your e-mail content. Many of my clients work on a 70/30 rule – that is, 70 per cent non-commercial useful content and 30 per cent about stuff they want to sell you. I would suggest that you go even further and aim for a 90/10 or 100 per cent non-commercial content. Providing useful content is the single best way to get your e-mail known and remembered, increase the likelihood of future e-mail opens and to drive traffic to your site. Once you have the site visitor, you have the opportunity to build trust, awareness and potentially drive someone along your sales funnel.

E-mail and the user journey

Once we understand the impact that e-mail marketing has on our potential user journey, and how effectively it can work as one of our digital branding touchpoints, we can start to really look at the great ROI that e-mail marketing can offer.

The importance of tracking code

When we look at our web analytics to try and understand where our web traffic is coming from and how it is impacting our bottom line, our traffic sources are an essential report. In Google Analytics these are found under the acquisition reports, and as you can see in Figure 9.2, they are broken down into some key areas. Organic search is traffic from sites such as Google (but not paid advertising from these sites), referrals are visits from other websites, social are visits from social websites and then we come to direct visits. Supposedly direct traffic is traffic that comes to your site when someone types your web address directly into their browser or has bookmarked your site and visits by selecting that bookmark. What direct traffic actually represents is visits where your analytics package has no idea where they have come from.

FIGURE 9.2   Acquisition reports in Google Analytics showing where website traffic is coming from

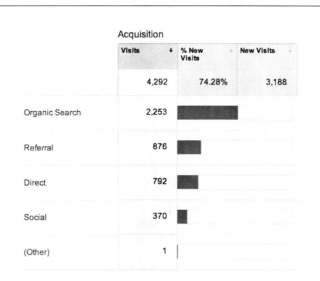

(Google and the Google Logo are registered trademarks of Google Inc, used with permission)

This is a really important thing to understand in regard to e-mail, because unless we add tracking code (which we'll explain in a moment and cover in more detail in Chapter 14) to the links in our e-mails, then people clicking on these links will show up as direct traffic and we won't be able to differentiate where they came from. So when we send out our e-mail campaigns, we will see an increase in direct traffic, but we won't be able to 100 per cent identify that as being a result of our e-mail.

Tracking code basically involves adding some information to each of our links, so that when a visitor arrives on our site we can use our analytics to identify exactly where they have come from (Figure 9.3 shows the Google URL Builder that allows us to generate this code). It is also possible that your e-mail service provider will give the option to automatically add tracking code, which can be a great time saver.

FIGURE 9.3   Using Google URL Builder to generate tracking code for an e-mail campaign

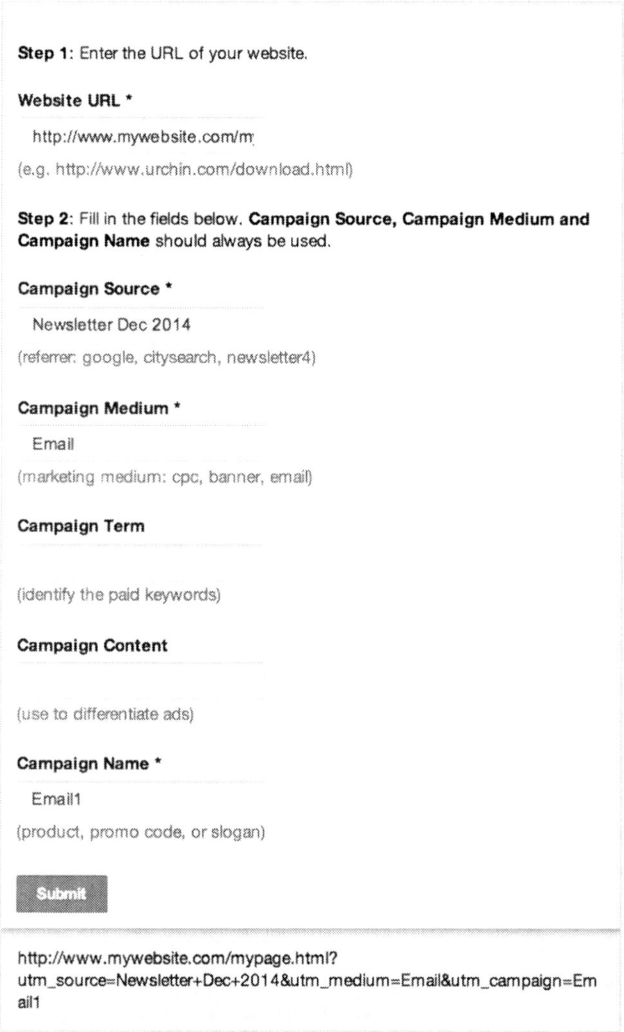

Step 1: Enter the URL of your website.

Website URL *

http://www.mywebsite.com/m

(e.g. http://www.urchin.com/download.html)

Step 2: Fill in the fields below. **Campaign Source, Campaign Medium and Campaign Name** should always be used.

Campaign Source *

Newsletter Dec 2014

(referrer: google, citysearch, newsletter4)

Campaign Medium *

Email

(marketing medium: cpc, banner, email)

Campaign Term

(identify the paid keywords)

Campaign Content

(use to differentiate ads)

Campaign Name *

Email1

(product, promo code, or slogan)

Submit

http://www.mywebsite.com/mypage.html?
utm_source=Newsletter+Dec+2014&utm_medium=Email&utm_campaign=Email1

(Google and the Google Logo are registered trademarks of Google Inc, used with permission)

A host of resources on analytics and tracking is collated on the website that accompanies this book: **http://www.targetinternet.com/ digitalbranding**

Going beyond last click

To understand how e-mail is having an impact on our overall digital branding, we need to understand where it fits into the user journey and how it is impacting the bottom line. We may expect someone to read our e-mail, then immediately buy our product or fill in our lead generation form (a form on our website that indicates a query or desire to buy). However, it is more likely that e-mail will be one of many touchpoints that build up our digital branding over time. For this reason, we need to consider the analytics results from our e-mail campaigns carefully and make sure we are going beyond the last click. We explore this idea in more detail in Chapter 14, but it is necessary at this point to understand each step of the journey that leads someone to carry out an action that we desire. For example, as we can see in Figure 9.4, there may be a number of different paths through to conversion. As we can see at the top of Figure 9.4, I may get an e-mail, some time later do a search trigger resulting from something I experienced in that e-mail, and then go on to carry out some form of online conversion. Alternatively, as we can see at the bottom of Figure 9.4, I might have just done a search and immediately converted. In both cases, if we looked at analytics from a 'last click' perspective, in both cases the source of the conversion would be seen as the search, as this was the last click before conversion. By that logic, we might challenge why we are even bothering with e-mail marketing and pull the plug on this activity. But if we do that we won't get the search that followed and we won't get the conversion.

FIGURE 9.4 Considering each step in the user journey and going beyond a 'last click' mentality

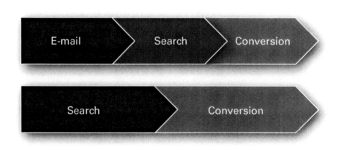

So in order to really get the most from analytics when we are thinking about e-mail marketing, we need to have tracking code in place and make sure we are looking beyond the last click. Happily, Google Analytics provides some excellent reports to allow us to do this in the shape of 'multi-channel funnels'. We look at this in more detail in Chapter 14, but essentially it allows us to see what channels were used by a visitor to our site up to 90 days before they convert. That is, what the different steps and channels are that were used in any of the user journeys that ended with one of our goals being completed.

Selecting an e-mail service provider

To really get the most out of e-mail marketing we have said we need to focus on relevance. In order to do that we need to think about segmenting our data, targeting the content, testing different elements of our campaigns and really making best use of the channel. To do that, and to make it easy to do, we need to select the right tool, and generally that will be some form of e-mail service provider. These tools generally work around three key areas: building, segmenting and targeting your e-mail list, building and sending your e-mails and, finally, giving you reporting on the results. Each of these areas can be extended to offer all sorts of functionality such as scheduling, automatic triggering and social media integration, all of which we'll explore more of later.

The key thing is: you don't want to get stuck with a system that limits your capability but you also don't want to pay for things you don't need. There are new ESP entrants all the time and many are very similar. To help you choose, some of the key considerations are listed below.

Enter the monkey

Mailchimp is a very popular and very low cost ESP. It has a very intuitive interface, loads of advanced functionality and is one of the cheapest ESPs on the market. They charge by the size of your list, rather than by how many e-mails you send, which can be a real cost saver if you are sending a lot of e-mails.

So what are the downsides? First, all support is done online, meaning you don't have an account manager you can call on. Also, it is a self-service system, and although the interface is very straightforward, it's down to you (although there is nothing stopping you from bringing in a third party to assist you). You need to pay using a credit/debit card, meaning if you can't pay this way then it's not for you. Also, if you need some form of customization or really advanced integration it may not be the right choice (although they do have an application programming interface (API) that lets developers do all sorts of things with the system.

I love Mailchimp, I use it for my business and I love the fact that it means I can test and learn quickly and easily. There are lots of other ESPs out there, but Mailchimp is often a very good starting point.
http://www.mailchimp.com

Requirements and functionality

There is such a dizzying array of things that your ESP could do, it is often hard to know where to start. A good place is by benchmarking the tools you are considering against each other in order to look at what functionality is offered. The list below is not a complete list of each tool and its functionality (as by the time this book is published it would already be out of date), but it provides a checklist of some of the key things you need to consider when selecting an ESP:

- **Requirements:**
  - How many e-mails are you going to send and how often?
  - How will your lists need to be segmented?
  - How much do you want to manage yourself?
  - Will you provide design or use a pre-created template?
  - What reporting do you need?
  - What is your maximum budget?
  - Do you need an account manager?
  - Do you want someone to do everything for you, including campaign analysis and planning?

- Do you need real-time reporting?
- Do you want a system you can log into and access directly?
- How do you want to get support – e-mail, phone, live chat?

- **Costs:**
  - Is payment calculated by period of time, by size of list or per e-mail?
  - What are the payment methods?
  - Are there any initial set-up costs?
  - Is there a minimum fee if priced per e-mail?
  - Is there a minimum contract period?

- **Functionality:**
  - Can I upload my existing e-mail templates?
  - Do they provide e-mail templates and are they any good?
  - Do they provide responsive templates?
  - Can I edit templates visually or do I need to edit code?
  - Can I add analytics tracking code automatically?
  - Can I integrate with my existing systems easily, such as CRM?
  - Do they offer A/B split testing easily?
  - Do they offer options for understanding what time of day works best for an individual e-mail or list?
  - Do they offer an API so that I can interact with the system with any software we may develop?
  - Do they offer an inbox preview to see how your e-mail will look on different systems when delivered?
  - Do they have a spam checker to show the likelihood of your e-mail being delivered?
  - What do they do to increase deliverability?
  - Do they have relationships with internet service providers and spam filter organizations?

 – Can I set automated triggers based on data such as birthdays and renewal dates?

 – Can I integrate the system into my site so that I can react to a user's behaviour on my site?

- **Lists:**

   – How can I segment my lists and what level of complexity of segmentation is offered?

   – Does the system do any automatic de-duplication when I upload a list? Am I able to upload my own lists and what are the rules in terms of how this data was collected?

   – Do they automate the double opt-in process?

   – How secure is my data?

   – Can I manage and edit my lists myself?

   – Can I build sign-up forms for my website and social websites?

   – What types of data can I collect and is there a limit to how many fields?

   – Can I cross-reference my lists against social media data to understand what social channels my lists are using?

- **Reporting:**

   – What reports are available?

   – Can I compare different campaign results?

   – Are there any benchmarking tools or data?

   – Do they try to compensate for the inaccuracies in 'open' rates (the percentage of people who open our e-mail)?

   – Can I access my reports at any time or are they sent to me?

   – Do they analyse the results and offer advice?

   – Can I see what content has been most popular?

   – Can I see the history for an individual e-mail?

Gaining opt-ins and building a list

In order to do any e-mail marketing we need to collect an e-mail list, and the rules on how we can collect data change from country to country. It is also not just a matter of following the rules, but really about following best practice in order to assure the quality of our lists and avoid annoying our target audience. Like many things in digital marketing, we tend to get distracted by volume when carrying out e-mail campaigns, and the question often asked after each campaign is 'How many e-mails have we sent?' and 'How many people are on our lists?'. What we should really be focusing on is the quality of our lists and the actual results our campaigns get. We actively don't want people on our list who don't want our e-mails, otherwise we are just creating a negative touchpoint that will damage our digital branding. I'm sure you can think of at least one company that keeps e-mailing you with irrelevant or overly sales-based content, and over time it creates a negative impression of that brand.

Best practice in regard to opt-in is to follow a 'double opt-in' approach – that is, to allow someone to fill in a sign-up form (more on that below) and then send them an e-mail that they need to click on in order to confirm their opt-in. This might sound like a slightly laborious process but most ESPs will fully automate this process for you. Also, the fact that the user has filled in a form and bothered to click on a link achieves two things: 1) they have self-qualified by showing they are actively interested in what you offer, based on the fact that they have actually made some effort to sign up; and 2) this sign-up process gives you actual evidence they have signed up, otherwise anyone could take your e-mail address and sign you up for any e-mail list!

Sign-up forms

Rather than trying to collect huge amounts of data at the point of sign-up, which will be a barrier to getting opt-ins, I generally recommend that you keep the amount of information you ask for initially to a minimum. You then have the opportunity to prove the value of your e-mails and then ask for more information by using surveys, questionnaires or polls on an ongoing basis. You also need to consider the types of data you may want to collect, whether you will really use that data and if your ESP is capable of storing it and using it. You may also want to think about how you are going to move this data between your ESP and your CRM (this topic is covered in detail in the next chapter).

The two key things that concern people when they are signing up to an e-mail list are: 1) what you are going to do with their data; and 2) how often you will e-mail them. Ideally, at this stage you will clarify both points with a statement along the lines of 'We will never pass on your details to anybody else and we won't e-mail you more than once a week'. You can also have a link through to your privacy policy that outlines clearly what you do with data, but in my experience very few people actually read these.

Buying in data and collection tactics

It is possible to buy in lists – but my general advice is don't! I should caveat that and say, if you can find a list on a niche group from something like an industry event or a controlled circulation magazine, you may have some success, but generally the results from bought-in lists are poor. Anyone on an e-mail list that is for sale is likely to be getting a lot of e-mail; also, it goes against our principle of focusing on data collected via double opt-in. There are plenty of other ways to collect e-mail data, and although building a list will take more time, the results should be very much better.

The first way is to have a website full of great content that is useful to your target audience. This will draw in search engine traffic and you can then offer access to even more content if they sign up to your e-mail list. This is an ongoing approach that should be present in all websites to allow interested parties to register their interest. It always bewilders me as to how many sites make it hard or even impossible to sign up for an e-mail newsletter.

The other, more direct approach is to use a pay per click (PPC) ad on a search engine or social media site to encourage sign-up. The basic process for collecting e-mail via PPC works like this:

- Step 1 – target the ad according to where it will be shown. For a search engine it will be by keyword; for Facebook by interests, location, age and so on; and for LinkedIn it will generally be around location and job role.

- Step 2 – create an ad that offers something useful for free on a relevant topic for the target audience. For example, if I've searched for 'digital marketing' you could offer me a free e-book, podcast, report or similar piece of content.

- Step 3 – when I land at your website I am presented with information on all the benefits of the offered content and then asked for an e-mail address in exchange for the content.

Not everyone is going to sign up, but those who do have qualified as being actively interested in the topic, and if you continue to e-mail them content on similar topics it will have a great positive impact on your digital branding.

Leading by example

A really great example of an e-mail company putting content at the heart of their marketing strategy is ExactTarget. ExactTarget are an extremely advanced ESP (in fact they offer a lot more than just being an ESP) and their marketing is centred around constantly publishing great research and content. It's well worth looking at the resources they provide, and they have some really useful e-mail marketing guides. As ever, I have no commercial connections to the companies I mention!

http://www.exacttarget.com/resource-center

E-mail sign up versus social connection

The value of an e-mail sign up shouldn't be underestimated, especially when you have grown your list organically as suggested, and have used a double opt-in sign-up process. If you consider this against gaining a Facebook Like or a Twitter follower, the effort involved to sign up to an e-mail list is much greater, and therefore those signing up are likely to be of a more qualified nature. This doesn't mean that those social media users who actually engage with you are less valuable than e-mail sign-ups, but offered a Like or an e-mail address I'd take the e-mail every time (but don't forget, there is no reason you shouldn't have both!).

List segmentation

As you build an e-mail list, you need to consider what differentiates the individuals on your list and what kinds of different content may be relevant to each of these segments. It is essential that your ESP allows you to collect data and add fields of information to your list in a way that will be practically useful for segmenting your lists in the future.

For example, you may want to send different e-mails to people living in different geographical locations – you will therefore need to collect and store that data. It could be that you want to store this data separately in your CRM system (we discuss these options in the next chapter), but for now let's assume we are adding more information to our ESP list. Different ESPs have different approaches and limitations to this, but increasingly many ESPs allow you to add a huge number of additional fields (in some cases an unlimited amount) that you can then use to segment and personalize your e-mail.

The benefits and risks of personalization

Personalization in e-mails generally often refers to the process of inserting personalized content such as your name, job role, company name or location into an e-mail. It can also refer to the process of segmentation or dynamically building content (these concepts are explored more below).

So if we are talking about inserting your name into an e-mail in order to personalize it, what actual impact does that have? Different studies show different results, and it certainly has to be seen in the context of your overall e-mail efforts, but there is generally a small increase in CTR. However, if you get the data wrong and insert the wrong job title or name, the damage will far outweigh any good you would have done. Therefore, only do this form of personalization if you trust the quality of your data 100 per cent.

We can segment our lists in a number of different ways, but we are generally talking about segmenting our lists based on collected data and by preference. That basically means that we have collected some information from an individual on our list and then use this to personalize their e-mail. This may be in the form of sending particular content, sending a particular format of e-mail or sending at a particular time or frequency, all based on the data you have collected.

This approach can be very effective in making e-mails more relevant and improving open rates and CTR. In fact, improvements of around 15 per cent in both open rates and CTR are entirely possible when taking this approach (Mailchimp, 2013).

Open rates and click-through rates

Two of the most commonly discussed statistics we get from our e-mail campaigns are open rates and click-through rates. It is worth understanding these in a bit more detail so that we understand where they are useful and what their limitations are.

Open rate tries to tell you how many people have actually opened your e-mail. I say tried because, unfortunately, due to the way it is calculated, it is inherently inaccurate. An e-mail is registered as open when an image in that e-mail has been loaded. So, you bring up an e-mail in your e-mail client, one of the images loads, and that tells the ESP that the e-mail must have been opened. This image is generally a single pixel image hidden at the bottom of the e-mail, often referred to as a web beacon. There are two problems with this approach. The first is that even if you open an e-mail for half a second and then delete it, as long as the image loads the e-mail will show as being opened. Although this is technically true, the open rate doesn't really paint a true picture of what happened. The other problem with relying on images being loaded in order to indicate an e-mail being opened is that when an e-mail is viewed by an e-mail client who doesn't load the images, you won't know it has been opened. It has been suggested that around 50 per cent of users don't see images automatically, which could mean some fairly unreliable data being reported as open rates.

However, this doesn't mean we should abandon looking at open rates. In fact, we are still using them as a benchmark – as at least we are comparing like for like from one campaign to the next or within split testing (discussed below). We just cannot rely on them as an entirely accurate representation of how many people open our e-mails.

Click-through rate (CTR) is the other key measure we tend to look at, and although a far more accurate measure, we can rely on it too much. Obviously, getting a click on your e-mail and driving a visit through to your website is great, but that is just part of the journey. It is entirely possible that everyone who clicks then gets through to your website takes one look, doesn't like the look of it and leaves immediately. You could therefore have a campaign with a 100 per cent CTR that was a complete failure!

So CTR is a useful measure but we then need to look at the visitor's behaviour on our site in order to really understand the true impact of our e-mail campaigns. So, for true commercial insights we will need e-mail reporting, web analytics and for goals to be set up in analytics. We also need to understand how these goals impact our business outcomes (and that is what Part Three of this book is all about).

This does highlight one of the potential weaknesses of e-mail marketing, however: even if you have the best e-mail campaigns in the world, if your website doesn't match that standard then your campaign won't be as effective as it could be.

E-mail templates and design

We could fill an entire book with discussions about e-mail design best practice, what works and what doesn't. The reason for this level of discussion is that how effective the design is will depend on your target audience, the e-mail client and device the e-mail is being read on, and a host of other factors. What that means is that we need to test for our particular list, and in fact we may find that different designs are more or less suitable for different lists and even segments of our lists. We explore all the different things that you can test for your particular list in the testing section of this chapter, but the key principles that every e-mail should take into account are highlighted here:

- **Header images above the fold**: don't place large header images at the top of e-mails. They push your content further down the page, and when images are switched off your audience will not see anything apart from a missing image.

- **Blocked images display**: consider what your e-mail will look like when images are switched off. Make sure you have a 'click to view online' link (most ESPs will add these automatically). Also make sure that all of your images have alt text, as for many e-mail clients this will display in place of the image when images are switched off.

- **Call to action placement**: consider where on the page your call to action will appear in various e-mail clients and try to keep it visible above the fold (before a user needs to scroll down to see the content). Bear in might that the bottom right, where many calls to action end up, may not be the most suitable place; you may need to have multiple calls to action.

- **Scanability**: users try to assess the relevance of an e-mail as soon as they open it – and decide if it is worth reading properly or not. Make sure your e-mail is scanable and that the key message comes across clearly and easily. Avoid large blocks of text, complicated layouts and poorly defined calls to action.

- **Unsubscribe**: every e-mail should have an unsubscribe link in the footer; this will generally be automatically inserted by your ESP.

- **Footer**: the footer of your e-mail should also include your physical postal address if you wish to be compliant with US e-mail regulations (CAN-SPAM act 2003).

Responsive e-mail design

Responsively designed e-mails attempt to adapt the e-mail according the device you are displaying it on and the size of screen display. This means that an e-mail will display differently on a smartphone, a tablet and a laptop screen. However, just as there are limitations in what we can do with e-mail design versus web design, there are limitations on the effectiveness of responsive e-mail design.

This limitation is because most responsive design principles rely on the support of media queries, a technique used to understand the size of a screen and then adapt things accordingly. Unfortunately, media queries are not supported by all e-mail apps. At the time of writing the most noticeable of these are the Gmail apps for iPhone and Android phones.

For a great summary of which apps do and don't support media queries take a look at the guide on the Campaign Monitor website: **http://www.campaignmonitor.com/guides/mobile/**

E-mail templates

There are a few options to consider when creating e-mails and the templates that you use. You can design your own templates from scratch, edit an existing template from your ESP, or use a template from another source. Each of your e-mails could be different, but in terms of brand consistency it makes sense to modify a particular template for a particular style of e-mail each time you send one. So, for example, you may have a newsletter template, a commerce template, etc.

Most ESPs will provide a set of standard e-mail templates that you can modify for your own use, and many also provide a visual editor that lets you edit these templates without any coding skills. Alternatively, you may need to edit your template code yourself and upload the HTML. You can do this yourself if you have the skills, or use a designer/developer to do it for you. There are a lot of ESPs that offer these kinds of services at an additional cost, or you could use a freelancer website such as Elance.com. Always remember, though, that e-mail template design is a very specific skill, and just because someone can design a website doesn't mean they know all the peculiarities of design for the wide range of e-mail clients.

The most important thing for your e-mail template is to make sure it displays properly on different e-mail clients and devices. To do this there are two options, one easy, one hard! The hard option is to

FIGURE 9.5 Litmus.com allows you to preview what your e-mail will look like on a wide range of clients and devices

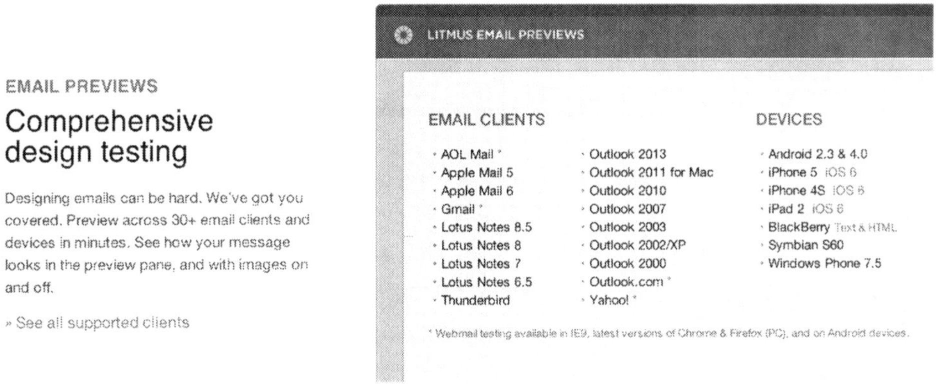

LITMUS EMAIL PREVIEWS

EMAIL PREVIEWS

Comprehensive design testing

Designing emails can be hard. We've got you covered. Preview across 30+ email clients and devices in minutes. See how your message looks in the preview pane, and with images on and off.

» See all supported clients

EMAIL CLIENTS		DEVICES
· AOL Mail *	· Outlook 2013	· Android 2.3 & 4.0
· Apple Mail 5	· Outlook 2011 for Mac	· iPhone 5 iOS 6
· Apple Mail 6	· Outlook 2010	· iPhone 4S iOS 6
· Gmail *	· Outlook 2007	· iPad 2 iOS 6
· Lotus Notes 8.5	· Outlook 2003	· BlackBerry Text & HTML
· Lotus Notes 8	· Outlook 2002/XP	· Symbian S60
· Lotus Notes 7	· Outlook 2000	· Windows Phone 7.5
· Lotus Notes 6.5	· Outlook.com *	
· Thunderbird	· Yahoo! *	

* Webmail testing available in IE9, latest versions of Chrome & Firefox (PC), and on Android devices.

manually test your e-mail template on every possible different e-mail client and possible device combination. This very quickly becomes an impractical task because of the number of possible options. This is why inbox inspectors were created, in order to simulate what your e-mail will look like on each of these different display possibilities. Many ESPs have these built in, but if your system doesn't you can use a system such as Litmus (shown in Figure 9.5).

Spam checking

We've already discussed the improvements in technology that are leading to the increased detection of spam e-mails. Unfortunately, the side effect of this is that your e-mail could be mistaken for spam by the many spam filters in operation – and never reach its intended destination. In order to minimize the chances of this happening you can use a spam filter testing tool. This will try to gauge the likelihood of your e-mail ending up in a spam filter and will point out the key things you may want to change in your e-mail.

Your ESP should have one of these tools built in but, if it doesn't, Litmus.com also offers this service.

Sending and testing

Once you have created your great e-mail content and built the perfect targeted list, you can start sending your e-mails. There are quite a few things to consider at this stage and a range of testing options are available.

Many ESPs will now allow you to carry out A/B split testing very easily, or you can manually split up your list in order to do this. The basic principle is that you take two segments of your lists and send each a variation of your e-mail, testing a particular feature of the e-mail (this could be subject line, copy length, etc). You then learn from these tests, work out which one got the best results and then apply this learning to the remainder of your list. For example, you could take two segments of your list, each consisting of 15 per cent of the total list, and run a test (making up 30 per cent of your list overall). You then learn from these segments and send out the better variation to the remaining 70 per cent of your list.

Open rate or click-through rate

When carrying out these tests, depending on what element of our e-mail we are testing, we will need to look to the open rate or the CTR for our results in order to judge which was the most successful. We can split these two measures as follows:

Open rate: subject line, time send, from address.

CTR: all variations within the e-mail content.

Once we decide what element of our e-mail to test, we also need to decide how long to wait after sending the initial two tests before we judge which is the most successful and send to the rest of our list. Figure 9.6 shows how easy some ESPs make this process.

Something you do need to consider, however, is the period of time you wait after sending your initial e-mails before you send to the remainder of your lists – and how this will impact your results. If you send out the test segments on a Tuesday and then send out to the remainder of your list on Wednesday, you will potentially skew

FIGURE 9.6   The easy-to-use interface for sending A/B split test campaigns using Mailchimp.com

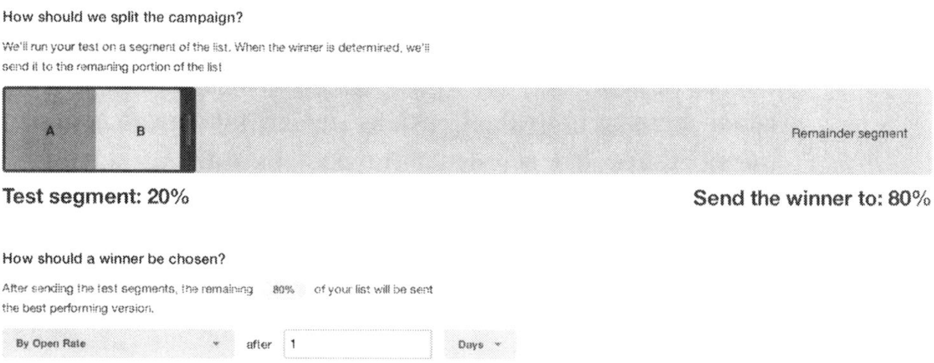

How should we split the campaign?

We'll run your test on a segment of the list. When the winner is determined, we'll send it to the remaining portion of the list

| A | B | | Remainder segment |

Test segment: 20%   **Send the winner to: 80%**

How should a winner be chosen?

After sending the test segments, the remaining   80%   of your list will be sent the best performing version.

| By Open Rate ▾ | after | 1 | Days ▾ |

your results, because people react differently to e-mails on different days of the week.

You could wait a clear seven days then send your follow-up e-mail at the same time of day and day of the week as your test e-mail, but even then you may find that things have changed over a week, due to the time-sensitive nature of your news story or similar.

There is actually no 100 per cent ideal solution to this problem, but what you should do is understand which days of the week work best for you and how different days of the week compare. You can then choose to send your test and follow-up e-mail on days of the week when your audience reacts in similar ways.

So let's consider the different elements of our e-mails and what we can vary and test.

Judged by open rate:

- **Subject line**: different subject lines with different tones can have a significant impact on your open rate and you need to understand what kind of thing works best for a particular list.

- **Time of day, day of week, month**: different groups react differently at different times, so we need to understand what works for a particular list and even an individual e-mail address. Bear in mind that time of day will be different dependent on where someone is in the world, so you may need to also segment by country.

- **From address**: the 'from' address can have a big impact on how likely it is that your e-mail will be opened. Should you e-mail from an individual, such as Daniel@mydomain.com or use an address like newsletter@mydomain.com? Again, you need to test for your particular list. However, you don't want to keep changing your 'from' address as it can cause problems with spam filters.

Judged by CTR:

- **Headings**: breaking up your content with headings can have a big impact on the ease of scanning your e-mails. The heading in your e-mail is therefore essential and a good area for testing different approaches.

- **Length of copy**: there are no absolute rules on how long your e-mail should be, other than not using long continuous blocks of text. You therefore need to break up your copy, but how long the e-mail should actually be is open for testing.

- **Image variations, size and placement**: fairly straightforward, but it can have a big impact on the results of your e-mail campaigns.

- **Call to action**: should it be in-text or a button? Should it be in different colours to ad placements?

- **General design**: the list could go on and on – and every visual and layout element of your e-mail is open to testing.

Dynamic content generation and rules

So far we have talked about building a list, potentially segmenting this list and then sending out content, with various testing opportunities. Many ESPs allow you to take your e-mail marketing a stage further and generate even more well-segmented and personalized e-mails. They do this by not only looking at preference data, that is data that has been collected from the individual, but by also collecting behavioural data and dynamically generating e-mails based on this.

This could be as simple as triggering one e-mail per month since the last e-mail click-through. It could, however, be a lot more complex and look at behaviour on your website then use this in order to adjust what content is sent out in an e-mail. If an individual looks at a particular product, why not send them an e-mail about that product? If they put an item in their basket but didn't buy it, why not send a follow-up e-mail? Based on what they have clicked on in the last five e-mails why not customize the content in the next e-mail, based on these interests? Different ESPs allow you to do different things, so it is worth considering from the outset the kind of dynamic personalization you may want to carry out. Some ESPs take this even further by thoroughly integrating with CRM systems, and we could even then start to look at the topic of marketing automation. We will look at these two topics in more detail in the next chapter.

Message banks and business logic

An increasingly common approach to solve the problem of sending too many e-mails on various different topics to the same individual is to use a message bank system. The basic concept is that we send a single e-mail that contains a number of different stories or pieces of content, but these pieces are selected and prioritized dynamically for a particular individual based on a set of rules we define.

The rules we define can be simple or complex, but they dynamically select content and place it into a particular order in a 'bank' of messages. This is only possible in some ESPs – and there are some key challenges to consider. If the rules are too complex, we may need too many pieces of content in the bank in order to meet all of the requirements we have set. It is also possible that some parts of our list never receive a particular type of content because other pieces are always prioritized. The key here is to build your rules carefully, not get too complicated and test all of the possible outcomes.

E-mail marketing conclusions

E-mail marketing is a hugely flexible area of digital marketing and can be an extremely effective part of our digital branding. It is also something that can be done badly very easily, so a suitable level of planning and resourcing is essential to get it right. Selecting the right ESP will impact everything you do in your e-mail marketing efforts, so select carefully and then make sure you are making full use of the various targeting and testing opportunities available.

CRM and marketing automation

10

We looked at e-mail marketing in the previous chapter and explored the great opportunities it offers in terms of personalization and the positive impact this can have on your digital branding. This can be taken a step further by integrating your e-mail service provider (ESP) with your customer relationship management (CRM) system, and there are even more opportunities when we explore the possibilities offered by marketing automation systems. We begin this chapter by exploring CRM systems and their relationship with e-mail and digital branding overall, then move on to the practicalities of automation systems.

Definitions and practicalities

Customer relationship management

CRM systems are basically where you store your customer data. As well as basic information such as contact details, the idea is that you store the history of your engagement with your customer, what marketing you have sent to them, any responses and so on. The systems are also not limited to customers and can be used to store information on potential leads, partners and suppliers. There are a wide range of suppliers of CRM systems and the breadth of what they can do is constantly growing and changing.

What you are aiming to do with CRM in regard to digital branding is to personalize any marketing you carry out so that each touchpoint is adapted and well suited to the needs of whoever you are talking to.

If you know what I have bought from you previously, my geographical location and various other things about me, you are able to make smarter marketing decisions. This means you can be more relevant and this enhances each touchpoint you have with your audience, thus improving your digital branding.

There are differences and similarities between CRM systems and what ESPs offer, but very often there is some blurring of functionality between the two things.

Marketing automation

Marketing automation is the process of not only triggering automated communications but doing this triggering according to a scoring system. This scoring system is what differentiates marketing automation from advanced ESPs, because many ESPs can do various forms of triggered communications already (such as sending an e-mail based on a user's website behaviour). Automation scoring allows us to set rules and thresholds based on both behaviour and information we have stored about someone. So, for example, I could decide to trigger a particular e-mail to you, based on what pages of my website you have looked at, how recently you looked at them, the fact that you attended a webinar last month, the size of your company and your job title.

Marketing automation is generally best suited to help with the sales process of complicated products where the buying cycle takes weeks, months or even years. This means it is generally applied to B2B products and services, although there is no reason why it cannot be used for more complicated consumer products such as cars.

Single customer view and bringing data together

One of the things that is required in order to use ESPs, CRM and automation systems effectively is the integration of these systems and the information they contain. The idea behind this integration is that of 'single customer view', which basically means that all of the information I have about you is accessible in one place so that I can make smart decisions.

Figure 10.1 shows the ideal scenario where we bring together all of our different systems so that we can use this information to make smart decisions. So, for example, I can send you the right information by e-mail based on your previous e-mail clicks, what you have done on my website and what you have said in social media.

FIGURE 10.1 The 'single customer view' achieved by bringing all of our sources of information together

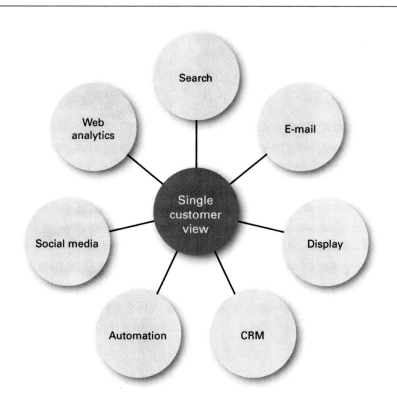

Essential and very difficult

The concept of a single customer view sounds like a great idea, and it is, but unfortunately achieving it is generally not easy. The reason for this is that what we are basically talking about is an IT project, and if there is one type of project that generally goes over budget and over schedule, it is an IT project. You may be wondering why trying to achieve single customer view has got anything to do with IT, and it is basically because we are trying to bring together systems and databases. If you are a small organization with little in the way of existing systems, or you are starting from scratch, this isn't a great problem. However, if you already have existing systems, you may find they are not compatible and need customization – and the whole thing is a general headache. My general advice on this, though, is that you should persevere, because I honestly believe that achieving this integrated view is what will differentiate between business success and failure for many organizations in the future. Let's explore why I believe that this is the case.

Smart marketing and agility

The environment we operate in is changing very quickly. Business and marketing continue to evolve at a dramatic rate, and our potential customers are all living in this environment. This has huge implications for our organization's need to test, learn and adapt quickly. Integrating our systems to achieve a single customer view means we can interrogate the data we have and hopefully use it to make smarter marketing and business decisions. This is hugely important from a digital branding point of view, because a company that is slow to react and continues to broadcast out messages, rather than personalize and have a two-way dialogue, will damage their reputation and erode customer trust.

CRM and ESP integration

In many cases it is perfectly possible to send e-mails directly from your CRM, without the need for an ESP. There are, however, a number of downsides to this approach and I would generally avoid it (although if you are using an online CRM such as Salesforce, many of the plug-ins that add e-mail marketing functionality are essentially like using an ESP).

The key downsides to using your CRM to send e-mails are around spam filtering and potential blacklisting. When you send from your

CRM, you are very likely to be sending from an IP address (how you connect to the internet) within your office (if that is where your CRM system is set up). The problem with this is that you don't have any whitelisting agreements or similar arrangements. A whitelisting agreement is something that basically says, 'we don't send spam and we follow best practice, so please don't block our e-mails'. These agreements are put in place with internet service providers and other organizations that are on the lookout for spam, and the advantage of using a good ESP is that they will have these in place. The risk is that when you start sending e-mails, someone thinks you are sending spam so blocks your IP address. Suddenly, no one in your office can send e-mails at all because they are all getting blocked, and you are not very popular!

IP blacklisting

If you are sending e-mails from your office IP address, and if this address is seen as suspicious by those organizations looking out for spam, you could get blacklisted. If you are seeing some of your e-mails not being delivered for some reason and are concerned about the fact that you may have been blacklisted, you can use a free service to check your IP address. If you are blacklisted, you can then contact the organization blocking you and they will have a process that you will need to go through to get unblocked. Visit **http://www.mxtoolbox.com**

The other reason to use an ESP is because of the generally superior functionality they have in regard to e-mail. They will be automatically set up to deal with things such as unsubscribe requests and bounced e-mails, whereas this may be something you need to set up when sending e-mail via your CRM if it sits on a computer in your office. ESPs also update their functionality on an ongoing basis and offer more reporting than you can get from a CRM system generally.

Data synching

If we have both a CRM and an ESP, the reason they need to be integrated quickly becomes clear when we look at the workflow (see Figure 10.2). We will take some e-mail data from our CRM, build a list in our ESP and send out an e-mail campaign. We will then have some reporting and details of who has unsubscribed in our ESP. Unless we then get this information back into our CRM, we are then storing information in two places and there are risks and limitations associated with this. First, there is a risk that we e-mail someone directly from our CRM who has unsubscribed via our ESP – and this is a breach of spam rules in most countries. The other problem is that we then don't have complete data in either system, so our future targeting will be limited.

FIGURE 10.2   The challenges and reasons for CRM and ESP integration

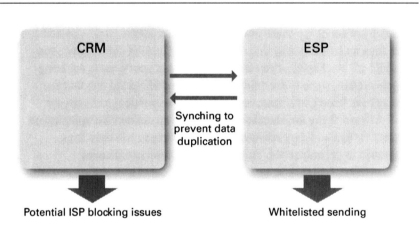

The solution is to synch back the data we collect in our ESP to our CRM and, as we collect more e-mail data in our CRM, we are able to import into our ESP without duplication. Most ESPs will offer a CRM integration service or provide an API (application programming interface), which means that a third-party developer should be able to do the necessary work.

If your CRM and ESP are in the cloud (that is, they are online services rather than something that is installed on a machine in your office), it is generally easier for the systems to speak to each other in real time. Otherwise you may need to do some form of hourly or daily synching. For this reason, if you use something like Salesforce for a CRM and Mailchimp for an ESP, both of which are online services and designed to work together, life will be a lot easier.

The alternative and far less ideal solution used by many organizations (because their systems are not integrated) involves importing data from a CRM system and using the ESP to de-duplicate this data. The ESP then works out which e-mail addresses being imported are new, which are duplicates and which have already unsubscribed. However, in this scenario data is not copied back to the CRM, so it is essential that no e-mails are sent from the CRM directly in case some users have unsubscribed.

If our systems are integrated we can then collect information via our ESP in the form of questionnaires and surveys and use this elsewhere in our marketing efforts via our CRM and in our future e-mail campaigns.

Advanced personalization and triggering

Many ESPs actually offer services similar to that provided by a CRM, allowing you to add many fields of data against a particular e-mail address for segmenting and personalizing your e-mails (this can mean there is sometimes a bit of blurring between functionality offered by either system). The more advanced ESPs will allow you to integrate your e-mail system with your website so that you can look at visitor behaviour. They can trigger e-mails based on all this different information and dynamically generate e-mails according to rules that you set.

Marketing automation

Marketing automation takes this idea of automatically triggering certain e-mails (or other forms of outbound communications) a stage further by trying to align it more closely with the sales process and adding the idea of lead nurturing and qualification. Once again, this kind of directly sales-related marketing would not generally be associated with branding but, as we have said, digital branding is created by the sum of every touchpoint someone has with your organization or product, and automation allows us to shape those touchpoints into a cohesive and personalized process.

The lead nurturing process

So, let's clarify exactly where marketing automation can fit and where it is and isn't useful. It is generally used when the buying cycle of a product is long or complex. The idea is that we are able to understand where someone is in the buying process, what their current motivation is, and therefore understand what the next steps should be. The next steps may be triggering some form of outbound communications such as an e-mail, or we may decide that this person is now a qualified sales lead, and we hand over to the sales team.

So marketing automation is all about nurturing and then qualifying sales leads via a marketing program in order to increase the quantity and quality of leads we generate and, in turn, sales (see Figure 10.3).

FIGURE 10.3   Marketing automation is used in the nurturing and qualification stage of the sales and marketing process

Automation scoring

At the heart of most automation systems is the concept of scoring. This scoring is used to qualify potential sales leads and decide when to trigger particular pieces of content. The scoring can be made up of a number of different factors, as highlighted below, and each system approaches things slightly differently. However, the core idea is that when a particular scoring threshold is reached an action is triggered.

> ### Marketing automation systems and resources
>
> There are a lot of marketing automation providers out there and the market can be complicated and confusing on first inspection. The three companies below all offer excellent marketing automation systems, and also provide huge amounts of educational resources on the topic on their websites:
>
> - Marketo: **http://www.marketo.com**
> - Eloqua: **http://www.eloqua.com**
> - Hubspot: **http://www.hubspot.com**

Implicit scores

Implicit scores are based on behaviour. We have highlighted a few of the potential behaviours that can be used to help with marketing automation, but remember that in order to use all these different measures, the systems that collect this information will need to be integrated with your automation system:

- Website behaviour:
  - pages looked at;
  - duration of visit;
  - downloads;
  - registration;
  - tools used.
- Events:
  - registration;
  - attendance;
  - sessions attended;
  - stands visited.
- Webinar:
  - registration;
  - attendance;

- voting;
- questions asked.

- E-mail:
  - opens;
  - clicks;
  - content clicked on.

- Social media:
  - likes/follows/+1s;
  - comments;
  - shares.

Explicit scores

Explicit scores are based on the information we hold about an individual or organization:

- Individual:
  - job role;
  - experience;
  - buying power;
  - location;
  - social influence;
  - demographics.

- Organization:
  - size;
  - revenue;
  - industry;
  - location;
  - relationship (customer, lead, partner).

Weighting

Each of these scores can then be weighted to decide how important they are to you or not. For example, the size of your company may matter to me very little, but your job title may be very important. The weighting will have an impact on when an action is triggered, so getting weighting right is essential to an effective automation campaign; we discuss below how your scoring and weighting will be adjusted and improved on an ongoing basis.

Negative scores

There may also be factors that we use to reduce scores as well. This can include implicit activities such as unsubscribing from an e-mail list or leaving a negative review or comment in social media.

At this stage, we also need to factor in time. For example, say you had visited my website, looked at some content, downloaded some things and that this had been sufficient to trigger a sales e-mail, but you then don't follow up or visit my website again in the next month. Once that month has passed, should you then get another sales e-mail? The answer is probably no, and we can protect ourselves from these kinds of situations by adding in automatic time-based score degradation. What we are doing is basically saying that you score points for certain things, but those things only indicate your interest or intent for a limited period of time, and we therefore lower the scores gradually over time.

More advanced automation options

So far we have looked at scoring an individual based on their behaviour, or information we know about them. However, in certain circumstances we may want to consider more advanced ways of analysing behaviour. For example, if I have a high-cost product that is complicated to buy. If I see an individual visit my web page for this product once or twice that may not be enough to trigger a follow-up. However, if 10 people at the same organization have each been looking at this product I would almost certainly want to follow up. So, by setting rules at an individual level and an organizational level I can spot this happening.

Different automation systems will offer different functionalities to achieve things such as the example just outlined. It is therefore always good to try and map out what kind of behaviours you are trying to identify before choosing a provider, so that you can make sure they offer the functionality you need.

Testing, learning and adjusting

A key element of any successful marketing automation project will be in getting your rules, scoring and weighting right so that you are nurturing leads and passing high-quality leads to sales. To do this, there are a few factors we need to consider.

One of the keys to a successful marketing automation project is to make sure both marketing and sales people are involved throughout the process of defining, scoring and weighting thresholds. You can generate all the leads you want, but if the quality is not high enough, none will convert and the process will have been a waste of time.

In order to build effective rules in the first place, a good starting point is to take a sale that you have already won and work backwards with the data you have. Would they have met your scoring criteria? If not, you clearly need to adjust things. This is known as a pre-deployment test. Once your rules are in place and the system is up and running, you can take a sample of the leads that you have qualified and passed to sales and see how many converted into actual sales. If they didn't, we need to examine our rules and see if they need adjusting to improve the quality of the leads. This is a post-deployment test.

A warning on marketing automation

On paper, marketing automation sounds like a great idea and the key principles are straightforward. However, achieving this in reality is not always easy. First, most of the systems involved are quite costly and the set-up process is something you will most likely need help with. This means there will be an initial set-up cost and project in most cases. If the systems that we use for e-mail, website content management and CRM are not directly compatible with your automation system, you are likely to have some initial integration challenges. Once these are overcome – and you shouldn't underestimate how difficult this can be to achieve – you need to define your rules. This can be time consuming and complicated, may involve lots of people and will need ongoing refinement. Also, this is something that should be considered a long-term plan. I say that from the experience of never having seen an automation project take less than 18 months from beginning to satisfactory outcome, as a lot of issues and challenges tend to be highlighted when you try to implement it.

CRM and automation conclusions

Integrating CRM and marketing systems to achieve a single customer view should be considered essential. It will give you the flexibility and ability to do smart marketing, which is essential to achieve great digital branding. Integration allows you to personalize the experience that your audience will receive and gives you much easier insights into that audience.

Marketing automation, on the other hand, is fantastic when implemented but is only suited to particular scenarios involving complicated products and services. It is a complicated process that needs the proper planning and resourcing to make it work effectively.

It is unusual to explore things like systems, data and infrastructure when discussing branding, but when we define digital branding as the sum of the touchpoints that someone experiences, it soon becomes clear why it has an integral part to play. We only need to take an everyday example to see how integral systems are to the user experience, what we think of a brand and how it can impact our likelihood to purchase. If I browse your website and look at certain products but don't buy them, and you then send me an e-mail listing similar products to those that I have been browsing, this can be an effective form of behavioural targeting. However, if I then buy a product but you continue to market that product to me, it will potentially have a negative impact. Both the positive and negative sides of this are possible because of the systems we use and the way in which we implement them.

From integration to transmedia campaigns

11

Before we move on to Part Three (Strategy and measurement), this chapter looks at how to bring together the tactical channels and technologies we've discussed to deliver cohesive digital branding.

Integration

It all starts with the idea of integration. We have identified our value proposition, aligned it with the target audience's needs, and focused on value throughout. Each of our channels have been carefully selected and we understand the potential journeys between each of these channels and how this may be a complex and non-linear process. We have identified our content requirements to deliver the optimal journey and delivered this in a frictionless way, regardless of what device or platform our audience is using. So we have integrated digital branding, right? Very nearly.

What is missing is the glue that makes it stick together, which in this case is data. We need to test, learn to refine things and to adjust. The environment we operate in is fast moving and fluid. Therefore our digital branding needs to be fluid and fast to adjust as well. That is why Part Three will be essential in order to create successful digital branding that will adapt and stand the test of time.

Multichannel marketing is dead

Multichannel marketing is the idea of delivering your marketing via multiple channels, which traditionally meant print, TV, catalogues and a website that said the same thing (or some other online/offline mix). It meant, for example, that a special offer on one channel was offered in the same way on another channel.

The reality is that if you are still trying to achieve this you've got it all wrong. Different channels are used differently and we don't want exactly the same from each. Digital means that we have dozens of different channels and we certainly don't want them all to communicate the same things. Yet that is not to say we don't want consistency.

Consistency of brand

The traditional idea of brand recognition is still essential. You need to be able to recognize my brand easily, so that the efforts I have made via my digital branding to make you understand my value proposition are remembered easily. Without that clear understanding of what the brand represents, the brand recognition is fairly pointless. Consistency in visual identity and tone only serves a purpose if the value you provide is clear.

Omni-channel marketing

Omni-channel marketing recognizes the fact that my target audience will want to engage and communicate with me across multiple channels in a way that suits them. It recognizes that each channel plays a different role in the user journey, and this role may change and adapt according to what the person engaging with it wants.

Bear in mind, though, that each user may start the user journey at a different point and jump many of the steps you expected. They may also revisit certain steps multiple times and leave long durations of time between each step. For example, I know that on average a lead generated on my website is done so by a visitor who has visited around five times. This means they have visited my site again and again, obviously finding something useful each time, before they finally decide to enquire about the service we offer. Without knowing this, I may have dismissed the traffic being sent to my site by various channels, as it never seemed to be converting into business. In reality, I just didn't understand the number of steps and complexity involved. Understanding this omni-channel approach is at the heart of truly understanding how different elements of your marketing efforts are contributing to your digital branding.

The approach to digital branding outlined in this section embraces omni-channel marketing with its focus on user journey and final outcomes.

Transmedia storytelling

I love saying the phrase 'transmedia storytelling' to people. They generally give me a bit of a smirk and then give me an 'I'm not buying any of this nonsense' kind of look, as if I've just expressed the silliest marketing jargon ever invented. However, it is real and is a fantastic opportunity to achieve incredibly powerful digital branding.

In reality, transmedia storytelling goes back to the very beginning of marketing. In fact, it goes back to the very beginning of language and communication. If I tell you a fact, you will probably forget it fairly quickly. However, if I tell you a story that communicates a fact, you'll most likely remember it. It brings it to life, gives it context and makes it engaging. It's human nature and it's how we've communicated since before we could speak. It's all about narrative.

Transmedia storytelling aims to tie together each of the channels and platforms we use – using narrative. This can lead to extremely memorable and engaging experiences. It also relies on great creative concepts and absolute attention to detail when exploring how the user journey can be understood and managed. Below is an example of one of my favourite transmedia campaigns – gamification.

Gamification

Gamification is the principle of encouraging behaviours by rewarding a user in some way. This may be as simple as posting a high score to a public leader board (and remember, this doesn't need to be limited to games, it could be for the most technical questions answered, etc). It can also take more complex forms, such as being the first user to discover a piece of hidden content, or unlocking hidden features when certain activities are carried out.

The key thing that makes gamification work is that the reward should be valuable to the user. This may be in the form of content or reward, and very often that reward can just be recognition.

For my favourite example of gamification, take a look at the video for Jay Z's *Decoded* book launch: **http://www.youtube.com/watch?v=XNic4wf8Ayg**

Integration to transmedia conclusions

The key to delivering great digital branding is to see how all of the different experiences that we are delivering fit together, whether that is via search, social media, mobile or any other digital channel.

In order for these to fit together, though, we need to test our assumptions, to adjust as things change and to have a constant commitment to improvement. To do this, we need feedback. This feedback takes the form of analytics, measurement and surveying our results, and that's what Part Three is all about.

PART THREE
Digital brand strategy and measurement

Introduction

What we have covered so far has suggested a new way to think about branding, plus examples of how you can start to implement your digital branding. What we haven't done yet is walk you through what I really believe differentiates traditional branding from digital branding. And bear in mind, your digital branding is almost certain to interact with offline channels as well, so it is not just about the channels being used – it is actually all about a different approach to measurement.

Effective measurement can help differentiate between branding as an excuse for something that can't really be measured, and exactly what role each piece of marketing activity played in the journey through to the completion of the user journey.

The common challenge for measuring the success of any branding activity, whether online or offline, is that our final conversion – be that a sale or completion of some other task – may happen via a channel that is disconnected from our marketing activities. For example, a sale on someone else's website, an order taken over the telephone or a booking made via a third-party supplier. What we aim to do in this section is show you an effective technique for bridging these gaps between our end objective and our marketing efforts.

This means that we can calculate the ROI of things such as social media, work out how our print campaigns have contributed, and put a value against all those e-mails we have been sending out. I'm not saying that it's easy, but it's entirely possible.

Traditional brand metrics

We discussed in Part One that brand is measured by asking questions and trying to judge what someone thinks of a brand – and trying to work out what this means with regard to potential sales.

There many different ways of looking at this, but generally we would take some sort of sample survey of our audience and see what their attitudes were before and after exposure to some form of marketing. This survey would ask a range of questions, and there are lots of different approaches, but fundamentally we are looking to answer these questions:

- Are you aware of the brand?
- Do you like the brand?
- Do you intend to buy the brand?
- If you have purchased, do you intend to do it again?

Essentially we are assuming that if we can get more people to answer positively to each of these questions, we are likely to get more sales.

What we can now do is take all of the data we have from web analytics and measurement tools and combine it with traditional surveying techniques to create a feedback process that allows us to continuously improve our marketing activity.

Sum of all experiences

If our digital branding is the sum of all experiences that someone has with our product/service/organization, then we should be able to look at how each experience has impacted the outcome of that overall experience. In this section we look at carrying out the following steps so that we can implement and improve effective digital branding:

- create a digital branding dashboard;
- bring in data from analytics and other sources;
- understand traffic sources and interactions;
- bridge the gap between online activity, offline activity and business outcomes;
- profile and improve.

Examples and supporting templates

We have created a number of templates and guidelines to help you implement your digital branding measurement. The most important of these for this section is the digital branding dashboard. On our website, we are always adding more case studies and stories of the challenges and successes of implementing the approaches outlined in this section. Most importantly, you'll find an example digital branding dashboard that you can use as a starting point and adjust to your needs. You'll find it all at: **http://www.targetinternet.com/digitalbranding**

Measuring digital branding

The traditional methods for calculating brand value generally make assumptions about the impact that the branding is having on some aspect of your sales. Many of these models are highly complex and not very easy to take action from. What we need to build is a framework that allows us to see the value of each of the pieces of our branding and gain insights that can be actioned to improve things.

Defining brand value and valuation

We need to be very clear what we are talking about if we discuss brand value or valuation. We are not talking about the value of a brand that is put onto the accounts of a business. It is actually more about understanding the effectiveness of your marketing and how the different parts contribute, more than it is about valuing a theoretical concept of a brand. We can, however, use this technique in combination with more traditional brand valuation techniques to either come up with more accurate figures or, if nothing else, prove their accuracy in a straightforward way.

Understand the value of every marketing activity

What I am suggesting here is that we should be able to calculate the value of every bit of our marketing activity and look at how it is contributing to the bottom line. This may not be a 100 per cent perfect approach, but it is a lot closer to reality than how we've been doing things up until now (if we have been doing any calculations at all). Those elements we called 'brand building' in the traditional sense basically meant that we didn't really know how much they contributed to the bottom line, but we were pretty sure they did.

Here I suggest a very practical combination of techniques that map out all of the steps of the user journey and see how they contribute to our end objectives. That way, every step is understood and nothing needs to be labelled as brand building. We are simply looking at different stages of our marketing activity and working out what brand impact it has.

For perfection we need a mind-reading device

A perfect approach to marketing is impossible, unless we can mind read. This is because even using surveying techniques, when you ask someone questions about why they did something they often have no idea, or recall things incorrectly. For example, if you ask someone why they buy a particular detergent, they probably have no idea. We can put this down to branding, but it still doesn't give us any detailed information. As long as there are humans involved, we try to read minds to some extent.

Digital shot itself in the foot

One of digital's greatest problems has been self-inflicted. In the heady days when digital marketing first started, we happily claimed that everything could be measured and that traditional offline marketing was dead. This was a little arrogant, to say the least. You can measure everything if it ALL happens online. So if you only market online and you make a sale online with a credit card, then you can measure most things. What it doesn't take into account is a scenario such as: the only reason your customer searched and found you on Google in the first place was because their friend told them about you in the pub the night before. Try to measure that. While we still have these kinds of problems with digital, we can nonetheless now measure a lot more than just pure online transactions.

TV has culture, digital doesn't... yet

If you spend a few million pounds on a TV campaign, you're probably quite likely to spend some money on finding out what it did for you. And in fact many agencies that work on TV will factor in some calculating of the effectiveness of your campaign into your overall costs. To be fair, if you're spending £2 million on a campaign, £10,000 doesn't seem like much to spend on calculating value. However, if you are spending £5 on a digital campaign, you're not going to spend the same again on finding out if you got ROI, because even if you did, you won't have done once you pay to work it out!

So we need to develop a culture of starting out with the concept that all digital activity will be measured – and that we can do this relatively easily and in a cost-effective way.

Filling the gaps

The most important thing we are trying to do in this final part of the book is to fill in some gaps. Does positive engagement actually lead to sales? We assume so but we don't actually know. Does more people being aware of your brand values mean you sell more? We assume so, but not necessarily. We will try to fill these gaps by demonstrating how measurement – and asking questions – can provide the answers.

Abandoning volume

One of the key problems with looking at volume-based metrics is that they don't give you an indication of what success actually looks like. You may feel that getting 10,000 followers on your Facebook page is a great success. However, if your nearest competitor has 500,000 followers, it's suddenly a very different story.

Volume is prevalent in social media measurement but also in other digital channels as well. We look at things such as how many e-mails we have sent, or the number of page impressions or unique visitors to our websites. These are not so much a measurement of success or failure but rather indicating factors that can lead to our actual desired outcomes.

Benchmarked social measures

To get away from purely focusing on volume-based measurement in social media we can do a number of things, and in the next chapter we look at an approach that ties in web analytics. However, even without getting into analytics we can do some simple things to give us much more practical information. We need to try and benchmark our measurement, and there are a couple of ratio-based social media measures that are easy to use (but fairly rarely used). In order to calculate both of these measures you need two of the social media measurement tools we discussed in Chapter 5: share of voice and audience engagement.

Share of voice is a great ratio for understanding where you sit in relation to your competitors, and for judging the success and reaction to your social media efforts. You will need a social media listening tool to calculate this, and for many channels there are free tools that will do the job.

You start by measuring the total level of conversation around the topic area you are concerned with. For example, a recent client of mine looked at the conversation around skin care. The easiest way to do this is to look at one channel at a time. So, for example, how many tweets there are around the topic of skin care within a particular geographic region (you can do this using the Twitter advanced search).

You achieve this by deciding on a set of keywords and phrases that you want to monitor, and then see the level of conversation on these phrases. You then repeat this process, but just identify the tweets that were specifically about (or mentioning) your product, brand or service. You will then have two numbers: one for total conversations and the other for conversations about your product. Divide the number of conversations about your product by the total number of conversations on the topic, and you have your 'share of voice' percentage. This may be very low, but you can continue your social media efforts and then take the measurement on a regular basis (normally monthly is sufficient).

Progress made in increasing this percentage gives you a more useful guide than just looking at the number of tweets or likes. The other great thing about this measure is that you can calculate it for your competitors. You then have a benchmarked measure that can give you an indication of how effective your efforts are, and how that compares to your competitors.

Audience engagement is another percentage that you can easily measure and benchmark against your competitors. I tend to look at it on a platform-by-platform basis so that I know my audience engagement for Twitter, Facebook, Google+, etc and can make efforts to improve this. Again, I normally measure this on a monthly basis.

You start by looking at the size of your overall audience on a particular social platform, such as Facebook or Twitter, and then consider how much of that audience is actually engaging with you. So, for example, if you have 10,000 likes on Facebook, and when you post some content you get 1,000 likes on that piece of content from your likes, then your audience engagement is 10 per cent.

We need to define what we mean by engagement. On a platform like Facebook there are multiple ways to engage as you can like, share and comment on a post. I would count any of these activities as engagement. With Twitter I consider a reply or a re-tweet to be engagement, and so on. Technically speaking, if the same user were to carry out multiple engagement activities on the same platform on the same piece of content, we should probably not count these more than once. In practice, however, it doesn't actually matter as long as you are comparing like for like. As well as taking this measure for your own social platforms, you can very easily analyse your competitors as well.

Benchmarking and business results

Although benchmarked measures don't relate directly to business results, they are far more connected to helping us achieve our objectives than just looking at volume-based metrics alone. Realistically, if you are targeting the right audience your share of voice is growing and your audience engagement is increasing – thus you are in a strong position. There is still a gap between this and actual sales, but we are getting closer.

The next stage is to connect these social media measures to our web analytics and business objectives, which we look at in the next chapters.

Measurement comes in many forms

We need to combine a number of different measurement techniques in order to really understand the impact of each piece of our marketing activity. This includes using basic web analytics, external search volume tools, marketing attribution tools and, finally, chopping up some data in spreadsheets. It is not as painful as it sounds, but the reality is that neither is it easy nor something that most marketers know how to do. This is one of the fundamental issues surrounding calculating ROI that we need to be clear on. It needs to be planned from the outset and is a process we need to repeat and improve.

CASE STUDY   Three Mobile – Dancing Pony

This campaign was launched in **February 2013**.

Background

Three Mobile has always been a fairly solid, middle-of-the-road brand when it comes to mobile. Until now the brand has been unable to achieve the recognition of its competitors and has had some negative press in the past. However, while Three Mobile may not be an innovator, it does seem to know its customers well and this insight led to the development of this fun and quirky campaign.

Objectives

Three Mobile's main objective was to connect with its audience and strengthen its strapline 'Keep on internetting' by providing content that it knew would appeal to its customer base. It also wanted to build upon the expected appeal of the campaign with an interactive element.

Strategy and execution

Three Mobile employed Wieden + Kennedy to come up with a concept that reflected the kind of content its customers liked to share. The brand's premise is based on the reality of why we access the internet and how we share and connect with each other. While other brands are telling us about all the cool and exciting things we can do with our devices and the web, Three Mobile acknowledges that more often than not we use the internet to look at videos of cute animals doing silly things. And this campaign delivers more of what we like.

The video featured a cute Shetland pony moonwalking to Fleetwood Mac across the Shetland Isles. To add in a level of interactivity, alongside the video was the 'Pony Mixer' tool, which allowed users to create their own version of the ad by choosing a different track and adding in special effects to the video. Users could then create their own unique dancing pony video and share it with their networks.

Results

The video received more than 3 million views in its first week and so far has racked up over 7 million views on YouTube. The video gained over 2,000 shares on Facebook and Twitter in its first week and has spurred a great number of copycat and parody videos.

Before the video was launched, Three Mobile's Facebook page contained mostly product updates with a few seasonal offerings that attracted somewhere between 10 and 200 likes per post. Since the campaign, Three Mobile has taken the premise and run with it and its feed contains much more of the same funny or cute animal shots that are now attracting anywhere from a few hundred to a few thousand likes per post, as well as hundreds of shares.

Three Mobile has clearly found its unique selling point (USP) and its customers are responding well to the new content, almost all of which is being gathered from elsewhere on the web. There is a great case study of the campaign on the Google Think Insights website and this claims a 27 per cent brand uplift caused by the campaign. The full video can be seen at: **http://www.google.co.uk/think/ case-studies/pony-case-study.html**

Comments

This is a clever and original campaign that clearly generated reach and engagement. What we don't have clear evidence of, though, is what impact it had on sales. In order to achieve this we would need to survey the potential audience to understand what impact the ad had on purchase intent and, importantly in this case, brand perception.

The reason that brand perception is so important in this case is down to how we make buying decisions about which mobile phone network to select. However, we need to be careful about talking about things like 'brand uplift' as this is a fairly loose term that can be used in a number of different ways. The campaign certainly achieved fantastic penetration and reported reaching 67 per cent of the UK audience, which is a great achievement. The next stage is to try and understand what direct impact this had on long-term sales.

Primaries and indicators

In order to do any effective digital branding we need to understand our potential audience's journey and understand how this can be influenced, improved and essentially lead to our desired outcomes. To do this we need to measure what is important – and learn from this and improve.

Beyond the last click

Analytics (explored in the next chapter) allows us to see activity on our websites and apps, and where that traffic has come from. It also allows us to track our desired outcomes, at least to some extent. What we need to be clear on from the outset, however, are the limitations of analytics and what it can't tell us.

Generally, web analytics takes a 'last click' approach. This means we look at some form of activity, such as a download, and see where the traffic came from that directly preceded the download. What this doesn't tell us are all the steps before that last step. Just because I came to your website from a search engine and then downloaded something, doesn't mean the search engine was solely responsible for the download. I may have visited your website 10 times before, from multiple sources over an extended period of time. This is what we really need to understand. Thankfully, by using some relatively new features in tools such as Google Analytics, this has become a lot easier.

Analytics also can't measure when our outcomes happen offline, such as when our sales come in over the phone or at a showroom. Does this mean that tracking in analytics is a waste of time? Not at all, it just means we need to be clear on what we want to achieve online and that this should be as close as possible to our actual desired outcomes. I define these online goals – that may not be our actual business objective but are as close as we can measure online – as 'primaries'.

As we look at the wide range of measurements we can take from analytics, surveying and other sources that we look at in the rest of Part Three, we need to decide what is important and what is not so important. I like to refer to these different types of online goals and measures as 'primaries' and 'indicators'.

Primaries are the key things that we can monitor online that are as close as possible to our business objectives. If you sell online with a credit card facility, then your 'primary' will be a sale. However, if you are looking for leads it may be forms submitted or calls made to a web-advertised telephone number. It could also be the registration for an event or the download of a very relevant piece of content. These are not our absolute business objectives in many cases, but the closest we can come online to achieving these. We will bridge the gap between these activities and our final objectives in Chapters 14 and 15.

Indicators are the things we can measure online that impact how many primaries are completed. In order to get a filled-in lead form, I need website traffic. In order to get that traffic I need a traffic source (such as a search engine or social media site). For the search traffic, I need to be ranking for certain search terms. For social media I need an engaged audience. Each of these things can be broken down into 'indicators'. For search traffic my indicators might be as shown in Tables 13.1 and 13.2.

TABLE 13.1 Indicators and data sources for search traffic

Indicator	Source
Traffic from search engine	Web analytics
Rankings for search terms in search engine	Web ranking tool
Page authority	SEO authority tool
Volume of searches for particular search term	Search engine data

TABLE 13.2 Indicators and data sources for social traffic

Indicator	Source
Traffic from social platform	Web analytics
% of engaged users	Social platform
Size of audience	Social platform

Digital branding dashboards

Each of these indicators takes us further towards our primary, and by bringing them together in a dashboard we can start to see where our challenges may be. Figure 13.1 shows how a single primary can have a number of different indicators and how these can be grouped by traffic source. We will explore where this data comes from in the next chapter on analytics, and extend this dashboard to include indications of how the channels worked together to achieve our primaries.

FIGURE 13.1 Dashboard showing a 'primary' and 'indicators'

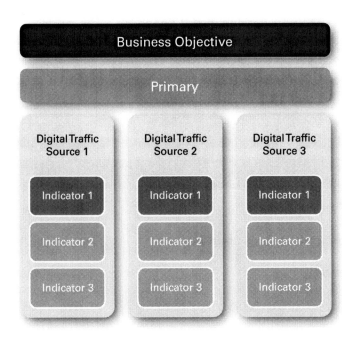

Dashboards and measurement

In order to properly measure and improve our digital branding efforts
we need to measure the right things. To help with this we have created
a digital branding dashboard that can help you work out what to measure
and what is important. It will also help you to work out what is of primary
importance and what is just an indicator.

See **http://www.targetinternet.com/digitalbranding**

The role of analytics

In this chapter we explore the huge opportunity that web analytics gives us, and how we use this as part of our digital branding dashboards. Web analytics means you will no longer have the problem of not having enough data with which to assess your campaigns. Your problem now will be having too much data and not knowing what to do with it. In most organizations I look at, they now have web analytics (this is an improvement on a couple of years ago), but the data is not used in an effective way. In fact, the most use that web analytics gets in the majority of organizations is a chart being held up once a month showing web traffic going up. This doesn't say why traffic is going up, how it could be improved further, or if in fact it is going up more slowly than the competitors. The data is just the starting point. To create effective digital branding we need to be able to analyse that data and use it to measure and improve our efforts.

The marvels of Google Analytics

Google Analytics, a free tool with over 80 per cent global share of the analytics market (W3Techs, 2013), has hundreds of built-in reports as well as a huge variety of customization options. It is constantly updated and offers a great deal of what many commercial analytics packages offer (and more in some cases). So one of the most common questions asked is: why is it free?

Google Analytics started out as a commercial tool called Urchin. This was then purchased by Google, repackaged and given away for free to help website owners improve their sites and drive revenue. Why does Google want you to make more money? Because then you are more likely to spend money on their advertising products, which generate 92 per cent of their income (Google, 2013).

There is in fact a paid version of Google Analytics – Google Analytics Premium – that gives you some of the things absent from the free version, such as an account manager, telephone support and service level agreements. It also gives you even more functionality and extended access to data and customization. However, it costs US $150,000 per year (this may seem like a huge amount, but actually represents good value when you consider what you get and the fact it is aimed at enterprise-level organizations).

Google Analytics global use and privacy

For some people and some locations, Google Analytics is not suitable. For example, it does not work properly in China because of data being blocked, leaving the country and its users unable to log in to read their reports. At the time of writing, there are legal challenges from Norway and Germany, which state that Google Analytics is not in compliance with privacy laws. In other cases, people just don't like Google or want to share their data with them. If you find yourself in one of these scenarios there are a number of alternative options. There are several excellent commercial options, the market leader of which is Site Catalyst from Adobe. There are also several free alternatives, including the excellent PIWIK. The core principles of analytics remain the same and the majority of the reports we discuss here exist in these other packages as well (sometimes under different names).

Throughout this chapter we focus on showing how you can use a tool like Google Analytics to help with every stage of your digital branding. We look at using the tools in practice and understanding how they can be used within our mobile sites and apps.

Setting up analytics

Most analytics packages use a technique called 'page tagging'. When you register for a Google Analytics account you are given a unique code that needs to be put on every page of your website. This code then sends information back to Google each time someone uses one of your website pages or app screens (see the box below for more on analytics in apps). This data includes a range of mobile-specific reports.

Google Analytics for apps

You can add Google Analytics to apps and get similar reports as you do for a website. Once you have set up an analytics account you add a new 'property' (a property is a website or an app). Once the app property is set up you are given a unique identifying code that needs to be built into your app. This is more complicated than just adding the code to every page of your website and will need to be done by an app developer.

The core thing to understand is that app analytics reports generally talk about screens rather than pages, as used in web analytics, but they are very closely aligned. There is also extensive reporting on 'events'. These are things that happen within a screen in your app without the need for another screen to load. You can also look at events in web analytics, but due to the nature of mobile apps they are more widely used in this scenario.

Core reports

Once you have your analytics code in place, your analytics package will start recording visitors to your website or app. These reports are broken down into a number of different categories, of which some of the core areas are highlighted below.

Real time

As the name suggests, these reports can show you people using your website or app in real time. You can track where they came from (search engine, other websites, etc), what content they are looking at and where they are in the world, among other things. One of the key things to remember about real-time reports is that they can be immensely engaging but an utterly pointless use of your time! Although the data is fascinating and it is thoroughly engaging to see who is using your website in real time, it is not easy to do anything useful with the data. It's great to see the instant reaction to an e-mail going out, or a social media campaign, but hard to take away any actionable insights.

Audience

This tells you all about where your audience is in the world and, very importantly, about the technology they are using to access your site or app. This includes data on mobile devices they are accessing on, and the operating system of those devices (see Figure 14.1).

Another useful report for understanding the user journey is the 'visitors flow' report (see Figure 14.2). You can use this to look visually at how people are travelling through your site. The great thing about this report is that it is easy to change the way that the audience is initially split up. As standard, you will see visitors from each country

FIGURE 14.1   The devices report not only shows the volume of mobile visitors but also the devices they are using

Mobile Device Info		Acquisition			Behavior		
		Visits ? ↓	% New Visits ?	New Visits ?	Bounce Rate ?	Pages / Visit ?	Avg. Visit Duration ?
		481 % of Total: 9.84% (4,887)	75.68% Site Avg: 76.80% (-1.46%)	364 % of Total: 9.70% (3,753)	77.13% Site Avg: 78.90% (-2.25%)	1.60 Site Avg: 1.53 (4.28%)	00:01:24 Site Avg: 00:01:29 (-5.36%)
1.	Apple iPhone	162	74.69%	121	74.07%	1.59	00:01:35
2.	Apple iPad	156	74.36%	116	77.56%	1.66	00:01:44
3.	(not set)	25	100.00%	25	80.00%	1.28	00:00:41
4.	Google Nexus 7	9	100.00%	9	66.67%	1.44	00:00:49
5.	Google Nexus 4	8	87.50%	7	87.50%	2.38	00:00:32
6.	Samsung GT-I9300 Galaxy SIII	6	66.67%	4	83.33%	1.17	00:00:09
7.	Samsung GT-I9100 Galaxy S II	5	20.00%	1	80.00%	4.00	00:03:23
8.	Samsung GT-I9305 Galaxy S3 LTE International	5	60.00%	3	80.00%	1.20	00:00:16
9.	HTC Flyer	4	25.00%	1	50.00%	1.50	00:00:10
10.	Samsung Galaxy Nexus	4	100.00%	4	50.00%	1.75	00:01:00

(Google and the Google logo are registered trademarks of Google Inc, used with permission)

FIGURE 14.2 The 'visitors flow' report shows how users are travelling through your site and where they came from

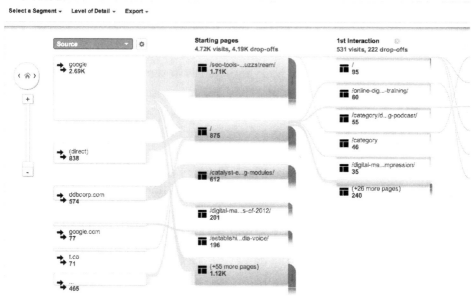

(Google and the Google logo are registered trademarks of Google Inc, used with permission)

and how they travel through your site, which pages they look at and where they exit. However, it is easy to change the initial segmentation from country to traffic source (search, social, etc). By doing this you can explore how visitors from different traffic sources travel through your site and see how their behaviour differs from one another. This can be useful in order to identify where each channel is fitting into your overall digital branding.

Acquisition

Acquisition reports (previously called 'traffic sources') show where your traffic is coming from and help identify which of your digital channels are helping to drive visitors to your website. You can view traffic from search engines, social media sites, other websites (called referrals) and direct traffic. Direct traffic is theoretically users who have typed your website address into their browser or clicked on a previously saved bookmark. The reality is that direct traffic just means that Google cannot identify where the traffic is from (more on this later when we look at tracking code).

Advanced segments and understanding the user journey

Advanced segments is an often missed but hugely powerful feature of Google Analytics that is incredibly useful when trying to understand the user journey and each touchpoint of your digital branding. It allows you to select a particular segment of your audience and then see all of the normal reports for that particular segment. You can also select multiple segments and compare these on the same report. There are predefined segments that you can easily select, or with a little knowledge you can build your own custom segments.

Another feature within acquisition reports allows you to look at your search engine traffic in more detail and understand the different search terms that are driving visitors to your site. By using these reports in combination with 'advanced segments', you can start to understand the different ways in which users from different locations, on different devices and at different times are exploring your content.

Unfortunately, a change in the way that Google reports now means that a great deal of the search terms that people use to find your site will no longer be reported on, and will just show as '(not provided)' (see Figure 14.3). This is because Google has decided that anyone searching on a secure connection (a website that starts https://) will no longer send the search term (which they used to find the site) to analytics. This is now the majority of searches.

Happily, there is a partial solution to this problem. If we go to the Search Engine Optimization menu option, we are given the option to connect our analytics to our Google Webmaster Tools account. Essentially this provides a lot more detail on what people are searching for to find us. The data is far from perfect, but it does provide a lot more insight than currently available from the keywords report (see Figure 14.4).

FIGURE 14.3   Using acquisition reports to look at search terms shows a large percentage of '(not provided)'

Keyword	Acquisition	
	Visits ? ↓	
	2,824 % of Total: 57.79% (4,887)	
1. (not provided)	**2,589**	
2. list of values	22	
3. moz seo review	17	
4. target internet	13	
5. social media success stories	5	
6. targetinternet.com	4	
7. top seo tools review	4	
8. qr contact data	3	

(Google and the Google logo are registered trademarks of Google Inc, used with permission)

FIGURE 14.4   Connecting Google Webmaster Tools to partially solve the problem of acquisition reports showing '(not provided)'

Query	Impressions	↓ Clicks	Average Position	CTR
	80,194 % of Total: 108.90% (75,000)	1,997 % of Total: 153.62% (1,300)	66 Site Avg: 70 (-8.48%)	2.49% Site Avg: 1.73% (43.97%)
1. list of values	15,000	600	3.9	4.00%
2. raven tools	3,000	30	7.2	1.00%
3. best seo tools	2,000	12	20	0.60%
4. core values	2,000	22	110	1.10%
5. best seo tool	1,600	5	17	0.31%
6. top seo tools	1,300	5	13	0.38%
7. digital marketing	1,000	5	250	0.50%
8. digital marketing training	900	16	15	1.78%
9. raven seo	900	5	8.1	0.56%
10. seo moz	900	5	36	0.56%

Show rows: 10 ÷ Go to: 1   1 - 10 of 3464 ‹ ›

(Google and the Google logo are registered trademarks of Google Inc, used with permission)

Under 'Acquisition' you can also examine any traffic you are getting from pay per click (PPC) campaigns that you may be running. If you are using the Google Adwords platform you can connect your analytics account to your PPC account and will then get full campaign reporting directly in Google Analytics.

Behaviour

As you can probably guess, behaviour reports highlight what users are doing on your site and which of your content is most popular (they were previously called 'content reports'). They will also show you how long users are staying on particular pages, and look at things such as bounce and exit rates (a 'bounce' is someone entering and exiting a website on the same page; an exit is just the final page in a website visit).

Not all bounces are equal

We generally assume a bounce is a bad thing. For example, someone arriving at your website from a search engine, landing on your home page, not liking the look of it and then leaving, is a bounce. However, someone bookmarking your blog because they read it every week, landing on your blog page, reading it for 25 minutes and then leaving, is also a bounce. The visitor still entered and exited your website on the same page. Therefore, a bounce isn't always a bad thing if the user has got what they wanted.

Another useful tool under behaviour reports is 'in-page analytics'. This allows you to actually see your web pages, navigate to an individual page and see the particular data for that page. It doesn't currently give you the option to view your site as if on a mobile device, but I have been assured that this feature is already in production.

Conversions

This is the single most important set of reports within analytics when looking at your digital branding, because it is the most closely aligned with your business objectives. A conversion is someone completing one of your online goals. As standard analytics will not have any goals set up, in order to get the most out of your analytics package you really need to set some up.

A goal is a user doing something you want them to do. That could be making a purchase, filling in a lead generation form, clicking on an ad, listening to a podcast, or any number of other things that may be aligned with your end business objectives. You can set up these goals within the admin functionality of analytics, and it is worth understanding the different types of goals you can set up:

- URL destination – a visitor getting to a particular page. Quite often a 'thank you' page, such as 'thank you for buying', 'thank you for downloading', etc. We know that if someone gets to one of these pages they have carried out an action and we can track this as a goal.

- Visit duration – you may decide that someone staying on your site for a certain period of time indicates they are using your content: this can help if your goal is awareness, for example.

- Pages per visit – you may decide that someone looking at a certain number of pages on your site is a goal. Always remember, though, this could mean that the user cannot find what they are looking for and are trawling through the content of your site to find it.

- Event – an event is something that happens within a page, such as someone clicking a link to an external website, or filling in a field on a form. We can also track these things within a page, but this requires additional code to be added to your web pages for each event you are tracking.

Once these goals are set up we will start to get goal reports. These show all the goals completed and can again be used in conjunction with advanced segments to isolate goals completed from particular traffic sources (see Figure 14.5).

FIGURE 14.5   Looking at a goal report with advanced segments in order to separate goals completed on mobile devices and desktops

Goal Completions	Goal Value	Goal Conversion Rate	Total Abandonment Rate	Podcast pages (Goal 1 Completions)	Email SignUp (Goal 2 Completions)
All Visits	All Visits	All Visits	All Visits	All Visits	All Visits
495	£0.00	10.13%	3.13%	493	2
Mobile Traffic	Mobile Traffic	Mobile Traffic	Mobile Traffic	Mobile Traffic	Mobile Traffic
49	£0.00	16.67%	0.00%	49	0

(Google and the Google logo are registered trademarks of Google Inc, used with permission)

Multichannel funnels

One of the limitations of goal reports is that they take a 'last click' approach. This means that if you look at the source of a report it will tell you what traffic source delivered the visitor to your site. For example, if you did a search in Google, came to my site and then filled in a form, the source of the goal would be a search. There is a problem with this, however: for example, if you receive an e-mail, visit my website, then a week later you do a search and then you fill in a form on my website – again the source of the conversion would be given as the search, but clearly the e-mail has also contributed in this instance.

This is where the very powerful 'multichannel funnels' reporting comes in. These reports tell you all of the different sources of traffic that contributed towards your goals being completed. So, for example, if lots of users are visiting via social media sites, but then visiting again via search and then completing my goals, these reports identify this for me. They show what percentage of all of my conversions have involved each of the different traffic sources, even if it wasn't the final click before conversion (see Figure 14.6). This can be hugely powerful in starting to understand how each of your different marketing activities is actually contributing towards your goals being completed (at the end of this chapter we explore how to combine the information from multichannel funnels with our other sources of information in order to help build more effective digital branding dashboards).

FIGURE 14.6   'Multichannel funnels' reporting allows us to start to understand the overall user journey in more detail

There were **484 total conversions**

~~~~~~~~~ Conversions: **484**

~~~~~~~~~ Assisted Conversions: **132**

Multi-Channel Conversion Visualizer

See the percentage of conversion paths that included combinations of the channels below. Select up to four channels.

Channel	% of total conversions
✔ ○ Organic Search	39.05%
✔ ○ Direct	33.68%
✔ ○ Referral	23.76%
○ Social Network	15.50%

Organic Search & Direct & Referral: 1.24% (6)

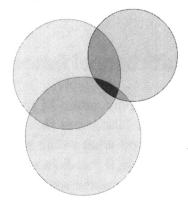

(Google and the Google logo are registered trademarks of Google Inc, used with permission)

Hands-on learning resources for analytics

Reading about analytics is one thing, but when you come to try out each of these reports you may need a little more help. I have listed here my favourite two analytics learning resources. Both are from Google and both are free:

Google Analytics IQ Lessons – these interactive online tutorials walk you through the core reports of analytics in a very clear way:
http://www.google.com/analytics/learn

Google Analytics YouTube Channel – this is an absolute goldmine of analytics tutorials and explanations. It also includes the excellent Web Analytics TV, featuring the hugely talented Avinash Kaushik and Nick Mihailovski answering lots of user questions about Google Analytics:
http://www.youtube.com/user/googleanalytics

Tracking code

In order to track some sources of traffic through to your site you may need to use analytics tracking code. This can be particularly useful if, for example, you are placing different versions of an ad on different devices. Tracking code is added to a web link and then, when the traffic source is shown, the details you have entered will be given. Let's walk through an example in order to make sense of this.

If I place a link in my e-mail that drives traffic to my website without adding tracking code, the traffic from the e-mail will show up as direct traffic. The reason for this is that when a user clicks on a link in an e-mail, Google doesn't generally know where that click has come from (unless we are talking about web mail). Therefore, to really understand our e-mail visitors we need to add tracking code to all of our links so that we can separate where the traffic has come from and analyse it properly.

Generating traffic code is very straightforward and, thankfully, Google gives us a tool to simplify things. First, search 'Google URL builder'. You will then find the Google URL builder (which is just an online form for generating tracking code). Enter the page you want to link to, fill in a couple of fields and it will generate a new link that includes your original link and appends the tracking code. Now if you add this to your e-mail, when someone clicks on the link it will be reported in Google Analytics as 'campaign traffic' along with the name you gave it and any other details entered into the URL builder.

This can be used to generate tracking code for e-mails, online ads, links in social media sites and so on, and can help you track a particular link and the traffic it is driving to your site. This is essential when trying to implement digital marketing dashboards, so that we can break down between different social media sites, etc.

Dashboards and analytics

In the previous chapters we explored the idea of using dashboards to better understand our overall digital branding. Much of the data for these dashboards will be found within our analytics, particularly for our primaries (normally set up as goals) and some of our indicators (such as volumes of traffic from a particular source).

We also need to see how these channels have worked together to achieve our primaries, and Figure 14.7 shows how primaries, indicators and data from multichannel funnels can be combined to visually give us an indication of what is and isn't working. The 'percentage contribution' is taken from our multichannel funnels to show how each traffic source has contributed to the particular primary we are looking at. Using multichannel funnels means that we need to have set up our primaries as 'goals' in analytics.

FIGURE 14.7   This dashboard shows a 'primary' along with a number of 'indicators' as well as showing how the traffic sources have worked together (by using information from multichannel funnels)

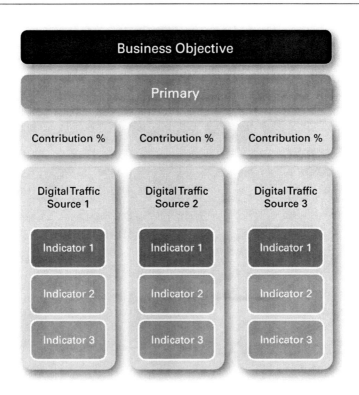

Analytics conclusions

Web analytics gives us a huge array of tools and information with which to better understand our audience and how they are moving towards completing our online objectives. However, unless all of our business is done online, we still need to bridge the gap between online and offline, and understand how our online activities are contributing to our overall business objectives. This is what we will look at in the next chapter.

Dashboards and analytics template

Don't forget, we have produced a dashboard framework that you can download in full and adjust to your own requirements to help track and improve your digital branding efforts: **http://www.targetinternet.com/ digitalbranding**

Bridging the gaps

15

The dashboard we built in previous chapters that shows us how each online channel has contributed towards achieving our primaries has some limitations. It doesn't actually tell us how many people who complete our primary actually go on to complete by business objective. Although a primary shows an action that is as close as possible to our final business objective, it doesn't mean this has actually happened. Also, the dashboard so far only factors in online but not any offline experiences.

Gap correlation

Gap correlation is a simple process of asking questions that show us the connection between our primaries and our final business objectives. We ask each of those customers who complete our final business objective if they completed any of our primaries. We then build a percentage, on average, of those who do. We can approach understanding this percentage in two ways: sample data and continuous sampling.

Sample data

We can take a percentage of those customers who complete our final objective and ask them about their primary completion. Once we believe we have taken a large enough sample (take a look at 'Sample size' in the box below for more detail on this) we can then use this percentage going forward to estimate how many people who complete each of our primaries will go on to complete our business objectives.

Continuous sampling

In this scenario, we continuously ask those customers who complete our objectives about their primary completions and feed this into our dashboard. This is obviously less prone than 'sample data' to giving us misguiding information that has occurred due to a change over time in the relationship between primaries and business objectives.

> **Sample sizes and confidence levels**
>
> We need to know how many customers we need to ask questions in order to get an accurate estimate of the relationship between primaries and business objectives. The number of customers we ask is our sample size. The larger the percentage of our customers we ask, the more confident we can be of our results. To do this effectively we need to work out what percentage of our overall customers we need to sample. A sample size calculator is provided on the spreadsheet for the digital branding dashboard, which you can download:
> **http://www.targetinternet.com/digitalbranding**

Keeping it simple – and the danger of selecting the wrong primaries

This approach to understanding how each of the different elements of our marketing are contributing towards our end objective is supposed to generate an easy-to-use dashboard that can show you what is working and what isn't. It is purposefully simple, but as set out below does not take into account a few factors.

Attribution modelling systems, such as that built into Google Analytics, try to look at the order in which different channels are used in order to work out their contribution. This model bundles together all the different possibilities of sequences of actions in order to try and create an actionable dashboard. Where this can go wrong, however, is when we select the wrong primaries. The risk is that no one is completing these, but they then go on to complete our business objectives. This would leave the dashboard fairly useless. For this reason I suggest focusing on a range of primaries initially so you can see which ones are the most important. You can then filter this down to those that are most suited to a simple dashboard. Remember, the aim of a dashboard when we are looking at digital branding is to understand at a high level how the sum of experiences we are providing is having an impact, rather than getting drowned in the detail.

Bring in offline channels and experiences

An offline experience includes such things as seeing a print ad, watching a TV ad, calling customer support or attending an event. What we need to do is understand how each of these offline experiences impacted the potential customers' 'objective intent'. What this means in practice is that when asked after this offline experience, did they state they were more likely to carry out the action that is our business objective (this is normally a sale but doesn't have to be) or not? The challenging thing here is to work out how to ask the question, and it will depend on what type of offline experience we are talking about. For a call to customer support, this can normally be achieved fairly easily. However, for a TV ad or print ad we need to get more creative, and normally this involves using the ads on a test audience. This test audience should be as close to our target audience as possible, but the question about buying intent may need to be a hypothetical one: do you think this would increase your likelihood to carry out our objective? For this reason, sampling offline experiences is generally far less accurate than for online ones.

This sampling gives us the 'intent percentage' and, for the sake of simplicity, we are seeing this as equivalent to completing a primary for our online experiences, as shown in Figure 15.1. These two are, again, not a like-for-like example, but nevertheless provide a good actionable dashboard.

FIGURE 15.1   Extending the dashboard to include the contribution of offline experiences

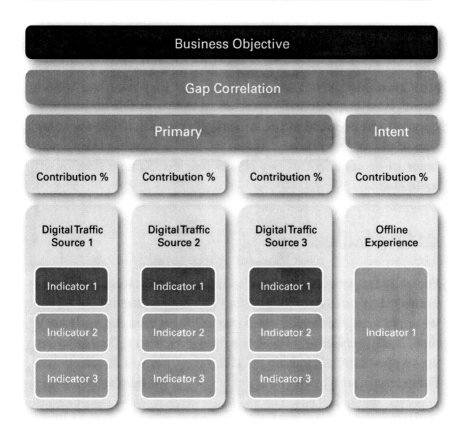

Avoiding the need for offline sampling

If the idea of getting together a test audience and asking them questions seems difficult and inaccurate, there is an alternative solution: simply try to drive people from the offline experiences to your website and then get them to complete an online primary.

We can see the flaw in this approach through an example, however. If I see a print ad that encourages me to go online, I then do a search in Google and arrive at your site. We will see this visit as being from Google rather than the print ad. The solution is to get your audience to use a specific URL to the ad (which many just won't do) or when they are completing the primary get them to indicate that they came from the ad – and then track this as a different online goal ad, therefore a different primary. It is not as simple to set up and you may need to get a developer involved in building custom forms, but it can add more accuracy to your data.

The next thing we need to understand is that of all the people who, after an offline experience, responded that they then had 'objective intent', how many actually went on to carry out this objective. This question can be asked at the same time as we ask about the completion of our online primary. Again, we need a suitable sample size in order to be confident of our results (see the 'Sample sizes' box for more details).

Offline indicators

For online experiences we have a number of indicators and these are normally layered in terms of how they influence each other. For example, we might have Facebook likes as one indicator, then engaged likes and then, finally, traffic from Facebook. However, with offline experiences we may just have one indicator and this generally will be volume based. For example, with a print ad we may just use the number of people we expect to see the ad, based on the figure given to us by the publication (or similar for a TV ad). With events and things such as customer service calls we may be able to add more levels of indicators. For example, an event registration followed by event attendance. Again, examples of this can be found in the spreadsheet version of the digital branding dashboard that you can download from our website.

A word on contribution

The contribution percentage shown in Figure 15.1 and in the downloadable spreadsheet needs to be clearly understood. For online it is showing the contribution of each traffic source towards the particular primary. For offline it is showing the contribution percentage towards buying intent. This is not a like-for-like comparison and the percentages of offline/online should not be compared. The aim of the dashboard is to allow us to adjust different elements of our marketing in order to try and improve the results.

If we want to understand the overall contribution of both online and offline together, and do a like-for-like comparison, we need to ask some different questions, as outlined in the next chapter.

Seeing it in action

Figure 15.2 shows the spreadsheet version of the dashboard in action, with a number of online and offline experiences. The spreadsheet includes tips for each sell, explaining what it is indicating and where the opportunities for improvement are.

FIGURE 15.2   Spreadsheet version of the digital branding dashboard

Objective	Sell Service						
Gap Correlation	38%					22%	9%
Primary/Intent	Lead Generation Form					Intent	Intent
Contribution %	58%	30%	25%	19%		38%	11%
Source	Organic Search	Paid Search	Facebook	Twitter		Event	Print Ad
Measure 1	Search traffic	PPC traffic	Facebook traffic	Twiter traffic		Attendees	Predicted audience
Value 1	8000	652	560	260		197	2500
Measure 2	Top 50 rankings	CTR	Engaged Likes	Engaged followers		Registrations	
Value 2	122	3.20%	1,040	768		280	
Measure 3	Site authority	Impressions	Likes	Followers		Enquiries	
Value 3	65%	20,375	13,927	7,940		340	

Dashboards and measurement templates

Don't forget, we have produced a dashboard framework that you can download in full and adjust to your own requirements to help track and improve your digital branding efforts. This includes help with tracking the gaps in your measurement framework and calculating the appropriate sample size needed in order to be confident of your gap correlation:
http://www.targetinternet.com/digitalbranding

The importance of asking questions

16

So far we have focused on understanding and analysing our digital branding by building an actionable dashboard. In order to bridge gaps in our data we have discussed taking sample data and keeping things as simple as possible. Although this is a very practical and hands-on approach, we need to make sure that it is accurate and reflects the actual impact our digital branding is having on our business objective.

The final step we can take to check this is to question those people who have already completed the final step in our business objectives and understand what different experiences shaped their impression of us, influenced their behaviour and led them to complete our business objective.

Confirming not predicting

Figure 16.1 shows how we can work in the opposite direction to when we use a dashboard: rather than predicting what the outcome will be, we start with the outcome and see how the online/offline experiences have impacted this.

This allows us to confirm what impact each of our marketing activities has had on achieving our business objective, and we can do this by simply asking some questions. The questions we need to ask are not opinion based but simply a list of tick boxes asking what experiences people had before they completed the final step. Then, by running this multiple times, we can start to get a picture of how important each of these experiences are.

FIGURE 16.1   Working in the opposite direction to a dashboard and understanding the contribution of each channel

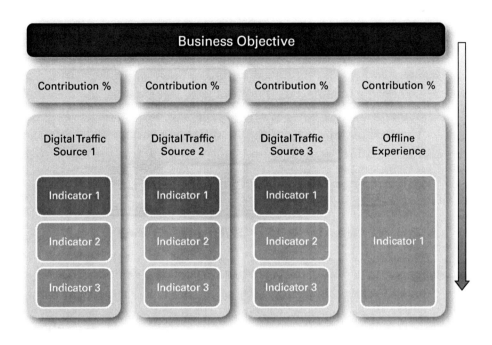

Sum of experiences

In order to ask the correct questions I need an exhaustive list of the different potential touchpoints/experiences of my customer. These could include online and offline marketing activities, customer services encounters, events and word-of-mouth recommendations. Once I have asked which of these experiences happened before the final objective was completed, I can then see what percentage of journeys that end in a business objective involved this experience. This is very much like the percentages we use when looking at multi-channel funnels in Google Analytics.

The sum of the percentages will normally add up to more than 100 per cent, as there will be a lot of overlap – but they will start to highlight for us which touchpoints are involved in the majority of objective completions.

Checking my dashboard

By carrying out this exercise and looking at how much each touch-point has been involved in achieving my business objective, I can potentially go back and check what my dashboard is telling me. This means that any assumptions or mistakes made in the dashboard can be identified and removed. This may mean changing the primaries that I am monitoring or looking again at my gap correlation.

This iterative approach means that not only are we optimizing our digital branding via dashboards, but we are refining the dashboards and feeding back from actual business results.

No one said it was going to be easy

Sampling data during the dashboard process and sampling from final results to refine this process may seem complex. However, in reality it is a fairly straightforward thing to do, but it needs to be built into your day-to-day business practice in order to minimize the effort needed to collect the data. Your call centre, customer service and event staff should be trained and familiar with collecting the appropriate data as part of their normal roles. Your offline ads should be orientated towards driving a feedback mechanism of some type.

Dashboards and surveying templates

Don't forget, we have produced a dashboard framework that you can download in full and adjust to your own requirements to help track and improve your digital branding efforts, with special fields for using surveying to help assess activity. We've included a space in this for double checking your assumptions.

http://www.targetinternet.com/digitalbranding

Conclusions

We have looked at digital branding as the sum of all experiences we have with a brand and we've tried to put together a process that much more clearly allows us to measure the impact of each of these experiences. Although there is no perfect process for trying to work out what motivates human beings to act the way they do, we can come a lot closer to understanding how each part of digital branding is contributing to the whole.

For too long, agencies and brands themselves have implemented marketing that has very little correlation to what the business objective is and how this will impact the bottom line in the long or short term. I am not arguing against innovative and creative campaigns that may not always work. In fact I actively encourage you to take some risks and try things out. However, I suggest doing this within a framework of measurement so we can clearly see what is working and what isn't and work out where to make adjustments.

Improve the branding and improve the process

As well as trying to have a clear view on why we are carrying out a particular marketing activity, within a measurement framework that allows us to see its contribution to our objectives, we also need to be open to improving the process. What I mean is that there is no one solution, measurement framework or dashboard that will suit every situation. We should therefore try to implement the methodologies outlined in this book, but also be open to adjusting and improving them as we learn from the process.

This book was actually all about 'big data'

'Big data' is not a term I have warmed to well, but essentially it is about dealing with masses of information and trying to make sense of it and come up with a sensible reaction. That is fundamentally what digital branding is all about: bringing together lots of information and understanding how the sum of small pieces make up the whole.

As technology integration improves, this should become much easier. One of the key challenges we face is that of integrating our sources of information, building a single customer view and making smarter analysis of this information. What we are trying to do with the process outlined in the measurement section of this book is to fix the gaps that currently exist in our systems and technology.

The sum of all experiences

Let's go back to the point that digital branding is about the sum of all experiences we have of something – and the impact this has. We should be able to see that by measuring more closely how each of these experiences work together to achieve our desired outcomes, we are basically understanding much more clearly what we do and the environment we work in.

Digital branding is all about making smarter decisions based on fact, and less on assumption.

REFERENCES AND FURTHER READING

Part One: Digital branding in perspective

IAB, 2013:
http://econsultancy.com/uk/blog/8859-iab-study-reveals-44-of-those-surveyed-use-mobile-to-respond-to-tv-ads

Mobile usage:
http://hbr.org/2013/01/how-people-really-use-mobile/

NewVoiceMedia, 2013:
http://www.callcentrehelper.com/poor-service-explodes-social-media-41455.htm

Chapter 1: What digital branding really means

American Marketing Association Dictionary, 2013
http://www.marketingpower.com/_layouts/dictionary.uspx

The Marketing Accountability Standards Board (MASB) endorses this definition as part of its ongoing Common Language: Marketing Activities and Metrics Project.

Chapter 2: Focusing on value

BBC, 2013:
http://www.bbc.co.uk/news/technology-24351904

Chapter 3: Considering the user journey

Digital Tourism Think Tank, 2013:
http://thinkdigital.travel/knowledgestream/mobile-drives-traffic-to-travel-sites/

Harvard Business Review, 2013:
http://hbr.org/2013/01/how-people-really-use-mobile

P&G, 2006:
http://www.pg.com/en_US/downloads/investors/annual_reports/2006/
    pg2006annualreport.pdf

Tipp-Ex case study:
http://www.google.co.uk/think/articles/fully-viral.html
http://lsjkhappy.wordpress.com/2013/03/15/case-study-of-tipp-exs-shoot-
    the-bear/
http://www.creativereview.co.uk/cr-blog/2010/september/tipp-exs-
    interactive-hunter-and-bear-film
http://www.ninjamarketing.it/en/2012/05/tipp-ex-one-year-later-the-bear-
    and-the-hunter-are-back/

World Travel Market, Jan 2013:
http://www.s-ge.com/sites/default/files/WTM_Global_Trends_Report_2013.pdf

Chapter 5: Social media

Adobe, 2013:
http://blogs.adobe.com/socialpractice/optimize-your-tweets/

Atlantic Wire, 2013:
http://www.theatlanticwire.com/technology/2013/05/facebook-mobile-
    ads/64802/

Marketing Land, 2013:
http://marketingland.com/twitter-60-percent-of-users-access-via-
    mobile-13626

Statista, 2013:
http://www.statista.com/statistics/191946/percentage-of-us-americans-
    concerned-with-privacy-on-facebook/

Techcrunch, 2013:
http://techcrunch.com/2012/04/12/google-analytics-officially-at-10m/

Telegraph, 2013:
http://www.telegraph.co.uk/technology/facebook/10030649/Facebook-
    under-pressure-to-deliver-on-mobile-growth.html

Chapter 6: Search

Cadbury case study:
http://www.fallon.co.uk/work/show/id/22
https://vimeo.com/21059963#

http://www.brandrepublic.com/news/784573/Gorilla-ad-works-its-magic-
   sales-Cadbury-bars/
http://www.campaignlive.co.uk/features/773064/
http://www.marketingweek.co.uk/cadbury-gorilla-ad-drives-uk-
   sales/2059658.article

Google, 2013:
http://support.google.com/webmasters/bin/answer.py?hl=en&answer=1061943

Researchscape, 2013:
http://www.researchscape.com/technology/130319_mobile_searches

SearchEngineLand, 2013:
http://searchengineland.com/mobile-seo-is-not-a-myth-8-popular-claims-
   refuted-141386

Chapter 7: Mobile

Affiliate Window, 2013:
http://econsultancy.com/uk/blog/62222-how-mobile-optimised-sites-drive-
   conversion-rates-and-aovs

Compuware, 2013:
http://offers2.compuware.com/APM_13_WP_Mobile_App_Survey_Report_
   Registration.html

Forbes, 2013:
http://www.forbes.com/sites/markrogowsky/2013/05/03/apple-as-the-app-
   store-nears-50-billion-downloads-the-birds-remain-angry-and-popular/

Google Mobile Playbook, 2012:
http://www.themobileplaybook.com/

KissMetrics, 2013:
http://blog.kissmetrics.com/loading-time/

Walker Sands, 2013:
http://www.walkersands.com/quarterlymobiletraffic

Chapter 9: E-mail marketing

Alchemy Worx 7, Debunking the Myths of E-mail Marketing:
http://www.alchemyworx.com/emailworx/2013/strategy/subject-lines/
   debunking-the-7-myths-of-email-marketing-%E2%80%93-infographic/

CAN-SPAM, 2003:
http://en.wikipedia.org/wiki/CAN-SPAM_Act_of_2003

DMA E-mail Tracking Report, 2013:
http://dma.org.uk/toolkit/email-tracking-report-2013

DMA National Client E-mail Report, 2013/14:
http://dma.org.uk/toolkit/national-client-email-report-2013

DotMailer Hitting the Mark 2013/2014:
http://www.dotmailer.co.uk/email_marketing_resources/download_
hitting_the_mark_201314.aspx

E-mail Analytics, Litmus, 2013:
http://www.emailmonday.com/mobile-email-usage-statistics

Mailchimp, 2013:
http://mailchimp.com/resources/research/effects-of-list-segmentation-on-
email-marketing-stats/

Percentage of e-mails that have images displayed:
http://www.campaignmonitor.com/resources/will-it-work/image-blocking/

SecureList, 2013:
http://www.securelist.com/en/analysis/204792293/Spam_in_April_2013

Chapter 12: Measuring digital branding

Three Mobile case study:
http://wklondon.com/work/view/three-the-pony-campaign
http://www.thedrum.com/opinion/2013/03/08/how-three-and-wieden-
kennedy-scored-viral-smash-thanks-dancing-pony
https://www.facebook.com/ThreeUK?fref=ts
http://www.youtube.com/user/three/theponymixer
http://wklondon.com/work/view/three-the-pony-campaign
http://www.youtube.com/watch?v=Ekr05T9laio
http://www.creativereview.co.uk/cr-blog/2013/march/threes-moonwalking-
pony

Chapter 14: The role of analytics

Google, 2013:
http://investor.google.com/financial/tables.html

W3Techs, 2013:
http://w3techs.com/technologies/details/ta-googleanalytics/all/all

WITH THANKS

There are many people who have encouraged and assisted me in writing this book and I have named a few of them here.

Firstly to the small and perfectly formed Target Internet team, Ciaran and Felice. Thanks to Ciaran for his incredible levels of enthusiasm even when wildly out of his comfort zone. Massive thanks to Felice for bringing together all of the case studies, so that I had time to actually sleep and eat. I also need to give the greatest thanks to our newest member, Susana, for her tireless work.

Again, a huge thank you to the very inspirational and talented Jonathan Macdonald for making the introduction that led to the book that led to this book! So many airport lounges, so little time.

Thanks to Allister Frost for his friendship and contribution to this book. Many thanks to Jess Butcher of Blippar for the generosity of her time in the frantic week before her maternity leave.

Thanks to Lauren Allchurch and Tom Ollerton from the incredible We Are Social for pulling out some fantastic case studies at short notice.

To all of the team at CIM who have supported and assisted in my career for many years by being both professional colleagues and great friends. Special thanks to Anne Godfrey for her foreword and trust, to Chris Moriarty for the best webinar double act in history, to Thomas Brown for the insights and laughs and to Renita Shwili for her continuing calming influence.

To the Econsultancy team for constantly challenging me, sending me to do interesting things and being professional and fun to work with. Special thanks to Chris Clapham for making that awful client call and to Alex Shaida for getting it all started in the first place.

And, finally, a massive thank you to all of you who have read this book, visited Target Internet, listened to the digital marketing podcast, followed me on Twitter and very kindly given me an audience to share my ideas and engage with.

Daniel Rowles

Also available by Daniel Rowles

ISBN: 978 0 7494 6938 2 Paperback November 2013

Order online at www.koganpage.com

Find out more; visit www.koganpage.com and
sign up for offers and regular e-newsletters.

INDEX

Page numbers in *italics* denote information contained within a figure or table.

CPSIA information can be obtained at www.ICGtesting.com
Printed in the USA
BVOW03s0047030414

349622BV00005B/27/P